A Brief Affair

Dale V. Foley

DALE FOLEY

PAGE PUBLISHING
Conneaut Lake, PA

First originally published by Page Publishing 2021

ISBN 978-1-6624-1011-6 (pbk)
ISBN 978-1-6624-1013-0 (hc)
ISBN 978-1-6624-1012-3 (digital)

Printed in the United States of America

This is my story of family and adoption; a reunion of birth mother and daughter; of love coming full circle after decades; of amazing coincidences, and how it brought two families together.

Acknowledgments

First and foremost, to Ann, who was so open and gracious with her family history and allowing me to tell our story.

To Richard McKenna, the brilliant marketing executive who came up with the perfect title, "A Brief Affair" and an eloquent ATA (About the Author). I am forever grateful to Rick.

To Gail Fine, a friend who happens to have an amazing eye for editing, came to my rescue and helped me see things I did not. I am forever thankful.

Last, but certainly not least, to my husband Frank for his listening ear and patience and Alex for just being the best son.

To all my friends and family who helped me along this personal journey, I thank you from the bottom of my heart.

Love to all.
Dale

Ann: Spring of 1953

College graduation is just days away, but I'm not sure I am ready to venture out into the real world quite yet. I loved these last four years. I worked hard and had a blast. I'm definitely ready to be done with all the studying, copious notes, and the thousands of index cards I used over the last four years to get by. Actually, more than getting by, I succeeded in every class. I did it, and I'm proud because a lot of the work was difficult for me. Mom and Dad will arrive in a few days with the old but dependable station wagon ready to pack me up and head home. I am amazed at the amount of stuff I collected in those four short years. I have two enormous crates filled with text books I can barely pick up and nobody wants any of them. Makes no sense to me. But the real question is "What do I want to do with my life?"

Yikes, those four years flew by, and I'm now realizing as a political science major, I am definitely not as marketable as my friends that majored in nursing or teaching. Two friends already have jobs lined up, but I never wanted to go that route. Political science seemed so much more adventurous, and I have always been interested in all aspects and eras of history and American politics.

My years at Duke were enjoyable. I joined a sorority, Alpha Phi, which gave me many lasting friendships. I was much more social than academic in high school, even more so in college, but I made it work, never wanting to disappoint my father. Duke is where he suggested I go, and that's exactly what I did.

Some of it was difficult for me as I struggled to keep my grades above average, a standard my parents would have expected. Thank God I had a close circle of friends that truly supported one another. Whether it be studying for an exam or writing a paper, there was always someone around to ask for help. I don't know how I would have managed without all of them. I hope we remain close friends, especially the girls in my dorm, but I do understand that distances have a way of separating people—just like high school when we all swore we would remain friends forever, but then life takes over.

Ann: The Early Years

I grew up in an area referred to as "the hill," in a small town in upstate New York called Olean just sixty miles southwest of Buffalo, as did my parents and paternal grandmother.

I lived in the same brown shingled, white-trimmed center entrance colonial house in a neighborhood with manicured lawns and white picket fences until I graduated from high school in 1949. My early school years were during WWII. It was the center of everything, always on everyone's mind. We collected all sorts of things for the war effort, bought stamps with our pennies in support, but I was really too young to fully comprehend the consequences of war. My father was too old to be drafted and was by then established in his banking career, but the war was a frequent topic of conversation.

I remember those years growing up with my younger brother Jim as carefree. We spent vacations during the summer in Canada, and I recall my father always drove but never more than thirty-five miles per hour as asked by the government to save on gas and tires. The rest of the summers were spent with friends from the neighborhood, riding bikes and playing in the fields behind our house. For lots of those years, we were not allowed to go uptown by ourselves due to the polio epidemic, which scared everyone. I was away at a one-week sleepover summer camp in Brewster, Massachusetts, on Cape Cod when the Japanese surrendered in 1945. Church bells could be heard for miles as I remember being quite emotional and wishing I was home.

My father, Robert Luther, was a good-looking man with dark-brown hair, always combed back, expressive blue eyes, and a genuine smile. He was always well dressed, frequently in a suit and coordinating tie, typical of a businessman of the era. Golf was by far his favorite sport, especially later in life; but he played football, baseball, and basketball in both high school and college. He graduated from Princeton University in 1925 and became a bank examiner in New York City before returning to Olean, taking a job with our local town bank, working his way up the ranks, and becoming president sometime around 1947. When I was growing up, my dad wasn't particularly strict with either of us but definitely expected us to do well in school. He never nagged or berated us but always helped when needed, whatever the situation. He was involved with most of Jim and my activities throughout our school years and was on the school board for as many years as I can remember. Dad's integrity, honesty and always being very involved in the community made him more than well respected in our town.

My mother, Mary Fitzpatrick, was pretty with delicate facial features, beautiful pale skin, and bright-hazel eyes. She was the fifth of six children to grow up in Olean, New York. She graduated from Syracuse University in 1925, started teaching home economics in Olean High School until she married my father in the summer of 1930. Shortly after they married, she left teaching to stay home and raise her family. She was the master of all things in our home, cleaning or organizing, shopping, and preparing simple but delicious meals, which I didn't appreciate until I was married myself. I don't recall her ever working, at least for a paycheck. She began painting, taking lessons, and becoming serious about art in those early years. She was naturally talented and studied under several well-known artists at the time. During my high school years, Mom spent summers studying in Provincetown on Cape Cod with the artist Henry Hensche. Over the years, she had many shows and became a talented and well-respected artist.

Sometime in the war years, an exact date eludes me as I was pretty young, Mom suffered a nervous breakdown. I recall it being stressful as she went away for several weeks but was constantly reassured that she was doing great from my father and aunts. They told me that Mom just needed a little time because she was exhausted. The only other thing I distinctly remember is that my dad took Jim and me out to dinner most nights which we both loved. She recovered and never had any incidents again that I'm aware of. My mother was also a first-class bridge player, and she, along with her sister Mildred, became a life master. During the 1960s, the two of them traveled up and down the East Coast to participate in bridge tournaments. She continued playing bridge until a year or so before she passed away in 1998 at the age of 98. My mom was a really good cook, although nothing ever fancy and I still cherish her Fanny Farmer's cookbook with her handwritten notes in the margins.

I especially loved my high school years. I was a cheerleader and involved in all sorts of after school activities. I enjoyed being a part of the school yearbook committee and equally loved being president of the student council. I have no doubt that all the extracurricular activities that I participated in helped me get into Duke.

Most of our family traditions were centered around Christmas. Each Christmas Eve, we would go to my maternal grandfather's house, whom everyone called Fitz, with all my aunts, uncles, and cousins. My grandmother died when I was just three years old and Jim was an infant. It was often mayhem but always such fun. Fitz gave each of his grandchildren a silver dollar every Christmas Eve as we ate cookies with soda pop. During Christmas morning, Jim and I could not go downstairs until Daddy called us, after which we opened presents from Santa Claus, and then my father made breakfast of scrambled eggs, bacon, toast, and squeezed oranges for juice. Dinner on Christmas Day was spent at my Dad's childhood home with my grandparents, Pop and Nana, and frequently my Uncle Larry and his wife, Aunt Nannie, with my two cousins. I recall it was pretty formal, always with an impeccably decorated table, lots of gold and silver Christmas knick-knacks everywhere, and a maid or more often referred to as a server to help with the dinner and clean up. I loved it—my brother, not so much.

Pop owned a men's clothing store in downtown Olean for as long as I can remember. He was always impeccably dressed and knew everyone in town by name and the name of their children and grandchildren. I remember my grandparents in the pew in front of me one summer Sunday at church as my grandmother kept shushing him to be quiet as he dissed the men in their old suits or mismatched outfits. I thought it was funny, but she clearly did not. I have wonderful memories of growing up in that small town with many cousins and friends still living there. My dad, along with his younger brother and only sibling, Larry, wanted nothing to do with my grandfather's retail business. They were both more career-minded and ambitious, both having attended private high school and then each going on to Princeton, four years apart. To my grandfather, education was important. More than important, it was necessary to achieve success and financial security. But I'm sure my grandfather was disappointed as the store had been in the family since before his grandparents. But he also understood the long hours needed to run such a business. Times were changing. My dad decided on a career in banking, and my uncle went into the insurance business.

My grandfather Fitz owned and operated the local *Olean Times Herald*, which he bought in 1911. My grandmother, who also was born and raised in Olean, met my grandfather while working at the paper and shortly thereafter, as I've been told, married. They had six children, my mother being the fifth. I grew up surrounded by many cousins and relatives, as most remained in the Olean area. We were closer to some more than others as my brother Jim and I were considered the young ones, having cousins in high school while we were still in early elementary school.

As the president of First National Bank of Olean, as well as a member of many local civic organizations, my dad had lots of connections, and I knew it wouldn't be that difficult to find a summer job after graduation. I needed to regroup and figure out what I wanted to do with my life and where I wanted to live. As a graduation present, my parents surprised me with a two-week European cruise with a small group of recent graduates. We were to travel to the United Kingdom, France, and Spain. I imagine it was going to be somewhat educational as well as fun. I was so excited I could hardly wait, and it definitely took the pressure of what my next step was going to be, a little reprieve of sorts. Grad school or interviewing for jobs could wait. My dad briefly suggested a semester at Katherine Gibbs secretarial school in New York City might be helpful in the job hunt. The cruise wasn't leaving New York City until late August, so I worked as a teller at my father's bank to make a little spending money. It was okay, actually pretty mindless. At least, I now know I won't be following in my dad's footsteps and go into banking. I actually filled out an application for Katie Gibbs for the coming fall semester, as I agreed with my dad that the secretarial school might be helpful in me locating a better-paying job. The fall semester started exactly one week after I got home from the cruise, which gave me plenty of time to pack up and head to New York City.

Funny being home again—comfortable, familiar, but boring. Really nothing had changed except me. After the cruise, I'd be heading to New York City and looking forward to a new beginning.

Mary Fitzpatrick Davis

Ann (circa 1947)

Ann's college graduation picture

Family Christmas card

Bob and Mary Davis

Mary and Ann (age nine months)

The Georgic

The ship named Georgic left port in New York City on a muggy but brilliant blue sky day in late August 1953. I felt like the luckiest girl as we headed to England, our first stop, spending many a day and night without seeing any land. As I recall, the seas were calm, and it was just such a fun adventure as I had never been on a cruise. The ship seemed massive and was a little disorienting, trying to remember how to get back to my room or to locate anyone of what seemed like a hundred dining areas. The tour group consisted of a total of twenty-eight students, five men and all the rest women. It didn't take long for all of us to feel like we had known each other for months rather than just a few days. We would gather at one of the bars, with a pool table and a Ping-Pong table and had the most amazing views of the wide-open ocean. Most, if not all, had graduated college and were looking forward to having some fun before settling down into careers, heading into the military, or continuing their education at grad school.

The very first day, I noticed this handsome guy from our group who I thought was quite energetic and a take charge kind of person. His name was John and he lived in North Carolina. He was tall, with light brown hair, big brown eyes, fit looking with a slim waist and broad shoulders. I think I was attracted to him because, generally, I was more reserved, and he was very outgoing and outspoken, always organizing some type of game or activity. He was what I would call the party guy. Roughly the third day at sea, a group of us were playing cards in the lower deck, and John came over and asked me if I wanted to take a walk around the ship with him. Me—not the gorgeous girl from Brooklyn or the funny girl from Long Island. No, he asked me. I was in seventh heaven as this handsome and charming guy wanted to be with me. From then on, we were inseparable.

It was my first time—my very first time. Obviously I was aware of sex, and I've kissed a few boys, but I knew this was going to be different. I remember being excited and a little nervous. He was so kind and gentle, and one thing led to another. I wanted to ask him if it was his first time as well, but I couldn't find the words. We made our way to his stateroom, holding hands, giggling, and frequently stopping to kiss in the long narrow hallways of this massive ship. Everything seemed to be going so fast. It was deep passionate kissing like I have never experienced. Both of my hands were held above my head gently with his as he pushed me up against the wall and kissed me. He seemed so confident and mature, which made it easy for me to reciprocate. Laughing and fumbling with keys, we made it into his stateroom. As we started kissing and slowly undressing, I recall not being embarrassed or frightened—just the opposite. I felt excited and pretty and wanted all at the same time, and I knew it was going to happen. There were so many mixed feelings as I wasn't exactly sure how this all worked. That might sound naive for a twenty-two-year-old, but it's the truth. We lay there for a long time after, and I felt safe and happy in his arms.

We were always together for the rest of the cruise but knew that it was coming to an end in just a few short days. I wasn't at all sure how this relationship was going to continue as we lived in different parts of the country. John living in North Carolina was going to be working for his dad upon returning, and I would be off to Katie Gibbs secretarial school in New York City.

As the ship was heading back to port, we had many conversations about the future. We had a wonderful, romantic time on the cruise, but it was pretty clear to me that I was not part of his future. He told me on more than one occasion that his mother wouldn't approve of me. I smoked and drank (as did he), but she would not have liked that. You would think I'd be upset, but actually, I wasn't. It was almost a relief. I liked John very much, and we had a wonderful time, but I didn't see myself settling down with him. Actually, I wasn't ready to settle down with anyone. However, we decided to keep in touch, to write letters, etc. We said our tearful goodbyes and went our separate ways on this cloudy and damp summer day in early September 1953. I just knew deep down, I'd never hear from him again.

MV Georgic

Manifest documents

Form 1416 TREASURY DEPARTMENT United States Customs Service UNITED STATES DEPARTMENT OF JUSTICE Immigration and Naturalization Service (Rev. 12-24-47)	Form approved Budget Bureau No. 43-R261	LIST OF IN-BOUND PASSENGERS (United States Citizens and Nationals)	LIST No. 4

Class __TOURIST__ from __SOUTHAMPTON__, __3 SEPTEMBER 19 53__ (Port of embarkation)

on __"GEORGIC"__ (Name of vessel) arriving at port of __NEW YORK 12 Sep 5, 19 53__

Line No.	FAMILY NAME—GIVEN NAME (1)		U.S. Passport No. PLACE OF BIRTH (2)	NUMBER AND DESCRIPTION OF PIECES OF BAGGAGE (3)	THIS COLUMN FOR USE OF MASTER, SURGEON, AND U.S. OFFICERS (4)
1	DE CHARMS AURELLE BRYN ATHYN, MONGOMERY CO. PENNA.	2d	62641 PENNA.	4	"- 273
2	DAVIS ANN 301 MADISON AVENUE, OLEAN. N.Y.	21 F S	153946 NEW YORK	3	
3	EVANS ARTHUR 9 WHITNEY STREET, WHITE PLAINS, N.Y.	70 M	WALES.	2	
4	ESTELMAN JOYCE 2974 MIDVALE ROAD, AVONDALE, CANTON, OHIO.	21 F	157880 OHIO.	3	
5	PEARIS LUCY 11 Dominick St., NEW YORK. N.Y.	58 F S	699242 ENGLAND.	4	
6	FINN SUSAN 1102 GREEN STREET, HARRISBURG. PENNA.	76 F	127352 PENNA.	2	
	FRUMIN ELINOR 1360 Ocean Ave., Brooklyn, N.Y.	25 F	136413 PENNA.	Did not embark. ...Purser	
7	FERLETER BEATRICE 1360 Ocean Ave., As Above Brooklyn, N.Y.	25 F	141037 N.Y.	5	
	FERLETER ALVIN As above	25 M	138655 N.Y.	-	
8	GILBERT AGNES 14 LENOX AVENUE, PATERSON, NEW JERSEY.	64 F	368229 ENGLAND.	4	
9	GARRATY WILLIAM 1031 WALNUT AVENUE, LONG BEACH. CALIF.	69 M	37294 ENGLAND.	4	
	GARRATY JENNIE ADDRESS AS ABOVE.	66 F	37294 ENGLAND.	-	
10	GILLIGAN MARY 381 GREENWICH AVE. NEW HAVEN, CONN.	44 F	95681 SCOTLAND.	6	
11	GILLIGAN JOHN ADDRESS AS ABOVE.	14 M S	95681 CONN.	-	
12	GILLIGAN JAMES ADDRESS AS ABOVE.	10 M S	95681 CONN.	-	
	GARGEIS IRMA 151 WEST 106 STREET, NEW YORK. 25.		91055 NEW YORK.	Did not embark ...Purser	
13	GROSS RUTH 58 BLANCHARD ROAD, SOUTH ORANGE. NEW JERSEY.	20 F S	76690 NEW YORK.	5	
14	GLOVER CARL A. 12 GREENE STREET. PAWTUCKET. R.I.	62 M	13637 ENGLAND.	7	
15	GLOVER GLORIA ADDRESS AS ABOVE.	51 F	13637 Okla.	-	
16	GILLESPIE PATRICK 678 EAST 138 STREET, BRONX N.Y.	47 M	70075 Scotland	9	
17	GILLESPIE BEATRICE ADDRESS AS ABOVE.	43 F	70075 Scotland	-	
18	GILLESPIE JOSEPH P. ADDRESS AS ABOVE.	10 M S	70075 N.Y.	-	
19	GILLESPIE MICHAEL ADDRESS AS ABOVE.	6 M S	70075 N.Y.	-	
20	GRIM O. LAWRENCE 520 CHESTNUT STREET, PERKASIE. PA.	20 M S	101714 NEW JERSEY	3	
	GEORGETOPOULOS JOHN 1037 BRYANT AVE., NEW YORK.		69684 NEW YORK	Transfered Sheet 57 Line 5 ...Purser	4

22 USC's

Form I-418
TREASURY DEPARTMENT
United States Customs Service
(Sea. 13-36-43)

UNITED STATES DEPARTMENT OF JUSTICE
Immigration and Naturalization Service

Form approved.
Budget Bureau No. 43-R061

List No. 10

LIST OF IN-BOUND PASSENGERS
(United States Citizens and Nationals)

Class TOURIST from SOUTHAMPTON, 3 SEPT., 19.5.
(Port of embarkation)

on "GEORGIC" arriving at port of NEW YORK 12 SEPT., 195.
(Name of vessel)

Line No.	Family Name—Other Name	U.S. Passport No.	Number and Description of Pieces of Baggage	This Column for Use of Master, Surgeon, and U.S. Officers
1	REED ERNEST 50 M M, 209 KAD—N ST., MADISON 4, WISCONSIN. Place of Birth: ENGLAND	157934	8.	279
2	REED EDITH 54 F M, ADDRESS AS ABOVE. ENGLAND	157934	—.	
3	SUNDELL ERIK 66 M S, 3048 KATLOCK AVE., CHICAGO, 13, ILLINOIS. SWEDEN	9293	4.	
4	STOPENKOFF LYDIA 23 F S, 1525 BELMONT, NEW HYDE PK. N.Y. NEW YORK	719308	5.	
5	SIEGS ROBERT 29 M S, CO 2D INFANT T.BRIGADE, STANFORD, CONN. NEW JERSEY	45768	2.	
6	SHELDON 15 F , NEW YORK, N.Y. NEW YORK		6.	
7	STONE JOHN 24 M S, 709 SUNSET L.., GREENSBORO, N.C. N.CAROLINA	177877	3. TRANSFERRED TO SHEET 50, LINE 16.	
	SH.. MARY, CONCORD, MASS. MASS.		PURSER.	
8	SCHILLER CHARLES 18 M S, 315 JACKMAN ST., Janesville, WISC. WISCONSIN	138981	2.	
9	SPUR AUDREY 51 F S, 8E INDEPENDENCE ST., SHAMOKIN, PENNA. PENNA.	57601	3.	
10	SHAFER DOROTHY 18 F , 404 PALMOLA DR., LAKELAND, FLORIDA. FLA.	155068	3.	
11	STEFFLET JOAN 21 F S, 904 MAIN STREET, STROUDSBURG, PA. PENNA.	107917	7.	
12	S.MRO. TERESA 24 F S, Box 1138, ESPANOLA, N.M. NEW MEXICO	98679	2.	
13	SANDERS WINIFRED 45 F S, GOODHILL RD., WESTPORT, CONN. R.I.	75175	5.	
14	S—— —SINGER 48, 61704 W. OLYMPIC BLVD., LOS ANGELES NEW JERSEY	109742	TRANSFERRED TO SHEET 31, LINE 15. PURSER.	
15	SIMS ELIZABETH 39 F S, 815 HEPBURN ST., WILLIAMSPORT, PENNA. PENNA.	43835	4.	
16	SWANSON DEAN 19 M S, 320 14th AVE. S.E., MINNEAPOLIS, MINNESOTA MINNESOTA	103029	3.	
17	SCOTT BEATRICE 62 F M, BOX 1022 ROUTE 1, NOVATO, CALIFORNIA ENGLAND—N.Y.	31701	4.	
18	SMITH WILLIA, 547—64th ST, BROOKLYN N.Y. MARYLAND	115100	BIG NOV EMBARK. Purser.	
19	SULLIVAN MARIE 46 F M, 130 W. 166th ST., N.Y.C. N.Y. IRELAND	82504	3.	
20	SULLIVAN THOMAS 9 M S, ADDRESS AS ABOVE N.Y.	82504	—.	
21	SULLIVAN ANNE 5 F S, ADDRESS AS ABOVE N.Y.	82504	—.	
22	S.KATS ARTHUR, 215 W. MCDOUGAL ST., MT. PLEASANT, MICHIGAN. NEW MEXICO	50541	TRANSFERRED TO SHEET 16, LINE 16. PURSER.	
23	SCHUTT MARGOT 21 F S, 202 ALLEGANY AVE., COUDERSPORT, PENNA. PA.	225921	7.	
24	TUTTLE SYLVIA 21 F S, 58 CLAREMONT RD., SCARSDALE, N.Y. NEW YORK	16417	5.	

21 XER U.S.C.

Printed and Sold by Devonshire Press
275 Varick Street, New York 14, N.Y.

24

John Stone
in the New York, Passenger Lists, 1820-1957

Name:	John Stone
Arrival Date:	12 Sep 1953
Birth Date:	abt 1929
Birth Location:	North Carolina
Age:	24
Gender:	Male
Port of Departure:	Southampton, England
Port of Arrival:	New York, New York
Ship Name:	Georgic

Obtained from Ancestry.com

Ann Davis
in the New York, Passenger Lists, 1820-1957

Name:	Ann Davis
Arrival Date:	12 Sep 1953
Birth Date:	abt 1932
Birth Location:	New York
Age:	21
Gender:	Female
Port of Departure:	Southampton, England
Port of Arrival:	New York, New York
Ship Name:	Georgic

Obtained from Ancestry.COM

Ann: Fall of 1953,
New York City

I was settling in nicely at the Barbizon Hotel for women in New York City and started taking classes. My parents were totally on board financially knowing that a secretarial school would help me gain a better paying job and the fact that the Barbizon was known as being quite structured—exclusively for women, weekend and weeknight curfews, and boys were never allowed in your room, even my brother. Most days, we ate breakfast and dinner together and had to sign in at the cafeteria entrance. Even though I had much more freedom at Duke, I still thoroughly enjoyed this time in my life. New York City was so vibrant and energized me.

Just as I predicted, I never heard from John. I sent him several letters with pictures from the cruise and got zero response. It was really okay with me. I honestly didn't spend much time pining over him as I was content, happy and carefree in my new life in the big city.

After arriving at Katie Gibbs, I reconnected with a classmate of mine from high school. His name was Chirp which I thought was rather funny but it was what everyone called him, including his parents. His real name was George. Chirp and I first met when his family moved to Olean in 1949 from Elmira, New York. We didn't date in high school, only sort of hung out with the same group of friends, an acquaintance rather. We lost touch when we both went off to college. Chirp had been drafted in the Korean War and was stationed at Fort Dix, New Jersey. We reconnected when he found out I was going to school in New York City. Even though we haven't spoken in nearly four years, we hit it off right away, conversing about high school friends and our hometown of Olean that never seems to change. We saw each other as often as we could, which wasn't a lot due to both our crazy schedules; however, any free time we always spent together. I was immediately attracted to him as I saw a maturity that I did not sense in high school. Chirp had grown into an intelligent, honest man that was quick witted with a dry sense of humor. Handsome, with sandy blonde hair, kind eyes, and always such a gentleman. I was falling for him big-time. John who?

Shortly after settling into the Barbizon, feeling comfortable, confident, and falling head over heels for Chirp, I discovered I was pregnant. I suspected as much as I was over two weeks late, and I was always very regular. I remember one night waking up with my heart pounding so hard, sweating, and gasping for breath as I had a dream that I was pregnant. Only it wasn't a dream. How could this be happening? My life was just all coming together. I felt so alone and isolated. I knew this was absolutely John's child, as I had never slept with Chirp. He was too much of a gentleman, never pushing to be intimate. John was my first and only. It was a horrible shock. I told no one and had absolutely no idea what I was going to do. I just let time pass in kind of a frozen state—totally in denial, totally paralyzing. I didn't know what to do, so I did nothing, pretending that my body was not changing. I felt absolute fear, shame, and panic. It was hard for me not to tell Chirp or my parents or anybody for that matter. I just didn't know how to get the words out… "I am pregnant."

Chirp and I continued dating until he left to go overseas at the end of December 1953 for a two-year tour, as he told me "to spy on the Russians." He had studied Russian at the Army school, where he trained in California. I knew Chirp was the one I wanted to spend the rest of my life with, but my secret was tearing me apart. When he proposed marriage at Christmas time right before he shipped out, I said yes, but I truly didn't know what I was thinking. Actually, I was praying that my "situation" would all just go away even though I knew that was never going to happen as I was a little over three months pregnant. Both families were excited, and although wedding plans were not being made as Chirp would not be back to the states for almost two years, there were lots of celebrations.

I had not told a soul. I just couldn't bring myself to tell Chirp and see the hurt and betrayal in his face. So I foolishly said yes to his marriage proposal and went along with the charade. I felt like I was living two separate lives—one engaged to the man of my dreams, planning our future and the other trying to survive this lie and total nightmare.

I received a letter almost every day from Chirp full of exciting things he was doing in the Army and all the things we would do when he returned and we were married. I found it hard to keep writing him letters as my belly grew larger and larger, and I felt more ashamed and isolated. In mid-March 1954, I went home for the funeral of my grandmother, who was in her late eighties and had been in poor health for a long time. I bought a one-way bus ticket and packed all my belongings in two duffel bags as I knew I would not be returning to Katie Gibbs or my dorm room at the Barbizon. I was seven and a half months pregnant and still had not told a soul.

I don't recall that moment entering my house and first seeing my parents and their reaction, as everything that day was kind of a blur. After the initial shock, my parents were amazingly supportive, and I wished I had told them much earlier. I couldn't stop thinking of the shame and humiliation I had put on my family, but neither my mom or dad reacted that way. My mother was especially supportive, not the reaction I had played out in my head for months, as she realized I had been holding this secret for a very long time. No recriminations of any kind. I was so thankful, and a huge burden was lifted from my shoulders. My dad promised that he and my mother would take care of everything, and he did just that. He arranged for me to spend the next two months with my uncle Larry and his wife, Aunt Nannie, at their home on Long Island, New York, until I delivered my baby. My dad arranged through a well-known reputable adoption agency in New York City to have my baby placed for permanent adoption. That was always my wish as well. I obviously knew my aunt and uncle, but under the circumstances, I was quite nervous and not sure how I was going to be accepted. They could not have been nicer, and I actually had a wonderful time with my Aunt Nannie, going to New York City frequently for outings of shopping and lunches. I was waiting and waiting and waiting for this baby to arrive and get on with my life.

I received a phone call from my mother while at my aunt and uncle's to inform me that my dad contacted Chirp's parents and told them the news. The engagement was off. That must have been incredibly hard, but he never said a word to me about it, ever. Nor did I have any further communications with Chirp. None.

The shame and guilt were too much for me to believe that Chirp would still want me. Damaged goods as they say. I took it upon myself to end any and all correspondence. My heart was breaking, but I did what I thought was my only option.

There were numerous times Chirp tried reaching out to me, but I had convinced myself that he would never accept what I had done, and I just needed to move on. Although heartbroken, that's exactly what I did.

Late morning, the first of June, I started feeling this pulling and tightening of my lower abdomen, and then suddenly, my water broke, or at least I hoped that's what was happening. Almost immediately, a contraction nearly knocked me off my feet. Intense, concentrated, and unfathomable pain in my lower abdomen had me doubled over. Aunt Nannie gathered my small, already packed suitcase, and we were off to Lenox Hill Hospital in the heart of New York City. She stayed with me as I settled into my room between contractions, and I made her promise she wouldn't leave me, and she never did. She stayed right there the whole time as I was somewhat comforted with the knowledge that she had already gone through this twice. I was frightened of this intense pain and the very real acceptance that I no longer have control over my own body. After what seemed like days but was only eight hours, I delivered a healthy baby girl on Tuesday, June 1, 1954, just before midnight. They seemed to whisk the baby away quickly but learned that was a normal protocol that they were cleaning her up and doing a fairly new procedure called the Apgar test. A nurse brought me my baby wrapped in a soft pink and white blanket. I took her in my arms and held her for what I knew would be the very last time. I gently kissed the top of her head, and through tears, I wished her a wonderful life.

The adoption was already in the works as I had previously signed over consent to giving up my baby. The agency and all the social workers made this difficult time in my life bearable—actually, more than bearable as they were all extremely compassionate, genuinely concerned with my needs, answered any questions, and never seemed to judge. There was no other option for me as I was never going to keep the baby, and honestly, an abortion never entered my mind. After spending another two weeks with my aunt and uncle, I was finally ready to go home. My family was supportive and encouraged me to get on with my life. In the fall of 1954, I did inquire about the baby girl named Virginia and was told that she was placed with a family who had adopted a little boy three years earlier. I never looked back from that day forward.

Dale: Summer of 2000

I finally received the letter. It seemed like weeks since I talked to the administrator from Spence Chapin adoption agency in New York City, but it was probably more like five days. I was looking for any updated medical information that might have been left in my file. I wasn't sure if there even was a file, but here it was, a three-page typed letter on their official letterhead. I remember sitting on the steps of our backyard deck on a beautiful but hot July afternoon, reading this incredible letter. I recall reading it quickly, turning each page carefully as if the letters were going to disintegrate and not fully comprehending all the details that turned out to be more information about *me* than I could have ever imagined. I read it at least three times before going in to show Frank, my husband of twenty-three years, who was working in his upstairs office.

It was so strange. These people mentioned in this letter were related to me. My birth parents, whom I had only ever envisioned as a very young couple, too young to have ever been able to take care of me, high schoolers or maybe early college. I never knew anything personal or genetic, except that I was adopted, until I received this letter. It was a crazy kind of excitement, not quite real, yet very real indeed. There wasn't any identifying information, such as names or places, and there was no updated medical information since this letter was dictated to and written by a social worker in June 1954. My reason for requesting this letter was due to some medical concerns for my then-fourteen-year-old son, which turned out to be a non-issue. Up until this very day, at age forty-six, I knew little about myself except my birth date, place of birth, height and weight at birth, that I was half German, half Dutch, and that my birth name was Virginia.

This was the letter I received:

July 12, 2000

Ms. Dale Foley
██████████
██████████

Dear Ms. Foley:

By now you should have received confirmation from the New York State Adoption Information Registry. Below is your non-identifying background information. I hope that you find it answers some questions for you.

Born in 1932, your birthmother was a 22-year-old, single, Protestant young woman of Welsh-Dutch-Irish descent. She stood 5'5" tall and weighed 115 lbs. She was described as a very attractive woman with a "collegiate" look about her. She was said to have had an engaging smile and quite a sophisticated manner. She had light brown hair, which she wore in a becoming short cut, large greenish-blue eyes, and a very fair complexion. She said that she was in excellent health, with the exception of suffering from hay fever. She had no other illnesses or diseases outside of the "regular childhood diseases". She graduated from college in 1953, majoring in political science. At the time that she first came into our agency she was attending secretarial school. She thoroughly enjoyed traveling and participating in recreational activities with groups.

Your birthmother provided the agency with information on her mother, your maternal grandmother. According to her, she was 51 years of age, stood 5'5" tall and weighed about 125 lbs. She had brown hair, grey-blue eyes and small features. She, too, was a college graduate, and taught home economics before marrying your maternal grandfather. In 1942, she reportedly suffered from a mild nervous breakdown, which your birthmother said was the result of exhaustion. She was under a doctor's care for six weeks and had no reoccurences at that point in time. Your maternal grandfather was also 51 years of age. He stood 6' tall and weighed between 165 - 170 lbs. He had black hair, grey-blue eyes and was described as quite good looking. He was a college graduate and worked as the president of a local bank.

Your birthmother had one brother who was 19 years of age at the time of your birth. He stood 6'1" tall and weighed between 145 - 150 lbs. He had grey-blue eyes and a fair complexion. He was a college student at that time.

Your birthmother described her family relationships in a positive manner, and said that she had always felt close to her parents and brother. She said that she was raised in a very protective and warm atmosphere. In school, she was an average student who worried sufficiently about her final exams, enjoyed a great deal of popularity, and participated very actively in social aspects of her college life.

Your birthmother provided us with the information we have regarding your birthfather. According to her, he was a 24-year-old, single, Protestant man of English-Scotch descent. She described him as quite handsome - standing 6'tall and weighing about 150 lbs. He had very light brown hair, brown eyes and a fair complexion. His facial features were described as small and he was a generally clean-cut looking young man. He graduated from college in 1950 and majored in business administration and economics. He was in the air force for a brief period of time and was working in a training program for a paper manufacturing company.

Unfortunately, very little information was known about your birthfather's family. Your paternal grandmother was a college graduate and was financially independent. Your paternal grandfather was deceased - "possibly of a heart attack". He was a college graduate and an owner of a chain of department stores, which he inherited from his father and grandfather.

Your birthfather had one sister who was 30 years old, a college graduate, and married with 2 children.

According to your birthmother, she and your birthfather met while they were both part of a summer student tour group traveling through Europe. Apparently there were only 5 young men in this group and 23 females, so your birthmother said that she was flattered to receive attention from your birthfather. She said that the thought of a shipboard romance made it easy for her to return his affections. While they had known each other for a relatively short period of time, she said that because they were together so much on the ship it made it seem as if they had been dating, or at least known each other for years. Their relationship intensified greatly on their return trip, and this is when they were intimate with each other.

After returning home, your birthmother had time to reflect on the relationship in a different light - particularly after she did not hear from your birthfather again. She mailed him photos of them on the trip and he did not respond. Shortly after this, when she discovered her pregnancy, she decided not to share the news with your birthfather. She stated that she felt that any efforts on his part would have come as a result of pressure regarding her pregnancy and she did not want to marry him under these circumstances. Your birthmother shared the news of her pregnancy with her parents and her aunt and uncle - all of whom showed her tremendous support and love throughout the pregnancy.

You were born on June 1, 1954 at 11:47 p.m. after a 40week pregnancy. The type of delivery was normal spontaneous and the length of labor was 8 hours. Your birth weight was 6 lbs. 10 oz., and you measured approximately 19" long. Your birthmother named you Virginia. You were described as a very relaxed and beautiful infant. You were very pink with velvety skin, quite a bit of dark blondish hair, blue eyes and a small rosebud mouth. Your birthmother was said to have regarded you with much admiration and emotion.

You were brought to Spence Chapin on June 8, 1954 by your birthmother and maternal aunt - directly from the hospital. You were placed temporarily in the home of a Spence babycare family. Your birthmother finalized her plans for you on June 28, 1954. You met your permanent family, the Iffinger's on October 25, 1954, and went home with them on October 27, 1954.

In the fall of 1954, your birthmother and her aunt sent a letter inquiring about your well being and asking for an update about your placement. A letter was sent to her including information about you, your adoptive parents and brother, and some photos of you.

I hope that this information helps to answer some of the questions you have about your background. I am interested in hearing your reactions and hope you will call me with any further questions you may have. Take care.

Sincerely,

Post Adoption Department

Baby Virginia, Summer 1954 in Foster Care

Wow! Oh wow! Oh *wow*!

So now I had all this new and amazing information about my birth parents and me, their parents, siblings, jobs, and interests. This was both exciting and terrifying, all at the same time. I was always curious about my heritage and birth parents, but it never became a driving force for me to search and attempt to find them. I was happy and content, and for reasons I could never pin down, I always believed that someone would try to find me, not the other way around. On some level, I was very relieved to know that my birth mother came from a good caring family. I think that most adoptees have at one time or another wondered if their conception was by rape or passion or something else. It was such a phew moment to realize that it was a shipboard romance and not something traumatic.

Dale: The Early Years

I always knew I was adopted and that my brothers were as well. It was never a secret. It didn't define me. It is just who I am, an adopted child, like millions of others.

I had a wonderful childhood growing up in the fifties and sixties in the town of Syosset, New York, a bedroom community of New York City. As I looked back, it was a "Father Knows Best," "Leave it to Beaver" kind of childhood. My mother, always nicely put together with hair done and just a little makeup, ran the house. She cooked, cleaned, and organized everything and was always around if needed. I have two siblings, a brother Curt, three years older and a brother Gregg, three years younger with me in the middle. We were all adopted from the same agency in New York City but from different birth parents. My parents, while choosing a name for each of us, used our birth names as our middle names. I always thought that was kind of special being the only thing we had to connect to our past. Besides the obvious differences in appearance, coming from three different biological birth parents, we really were all very different. Curt was labeled the smart one, Gregg, the athletic one and me the social one. Not sure where those labels came from, but it was a perspective that each of us remembers. I'd like to think each of us has evolved into more than that.

Nature versus nurture is an interesting question. So much has been written about it, but I'm not convinced there is a clear-cut line that separates the two. While nature is only part of the person, nurture is equally important to one's development and personality. Curt, Gregg and I were raised in the same house with the same parents, and each of us could not be any different. Although, I do believe that is also true for a lot of families that are genetically related. When it comes down to it, we really are all very unique individuals, no matter the circumstances of our birth.

The one true thing the three of us had in common was that someone was unwilling or unable to take care of us. My mother used to say that we were special, that we were chosen. It is a nice sentiment, but I think it is a crock of shit just to make adoptees feel less unwanted.

Curt, being somewhat serious and honest to a fault, always had a chip on his shoulder, which grew as he did. Unlike Gregg or myself, Curt was adopted at eighteen months of age, having spent that year and a half with his biological parents, and for reasons unknown, he was given up for adoption. Very few could remember much of anything at that tender young age, but after a year and a half, you have certainly bonded with those people. That would have to affect you somehow, some way. That is the ultimate "Primal Wound," defined as "severing the connection between infant and birthmother." Infants taken away from the only sight, sound, and smell they have ever known. Even newborns can feel something is wrong and actually grieve. This can manifest itself in severe and long lasting negative ways for so many adoptees.

Curt was smart, quick-witted, a slob, and goofy at times. I remember him coming to visit me at college and walking into my dorm house with a six-pack of Budweiser and a package of hot dogs. That was it. I'm not sure what he thought I was going to do with the hot dogs but stated loudly, "Anybody want some brewskis and dogs?"

Gregg, being three years younger, I somehow felt a little protective of him while he was always running around with some kind of ball in his hand. We all got along for the most part, obviously had our arguments and differences but just normal sibling rivalries. My parents hated when we fought and demanded that we always had each other's back. You were never ever to make fun of one another. My brothers would call me four-eyes sometimes, as I wore glasses. It never phased me, but it bothered my father a lot. After overhearing one of my brothers referring to me as four eyes, at dinner that evening we had a rather serious conversation about bullying. I was only about eight or nine but vividly recall the discussion went deeper than just my brothers teasing me. My father stated in his low serious voice how he felt it was cruel and unfair to attack someone just for a laugh, especially in a group setting. It was my first memorable impression of the kindness and integrity that I later came to realize about my dad. We debated what was funny and appropriate or hurtful and mean-spirited, never coming to a definitive answer.

As a family we rarely talked about adoption. It wasn't taboo or off limits, but it seldom came up. I can't speak for my brothers, but I didn't often have thoughts of my own adoption. Obviously, there were times throughout my childhood when questions crossed my mind, especially around my birthday. Was there someone out there thinking about me today? Occasionally, someone would say that my father and I looked alike, and we would just smile and share a knowing nod. We both had big brown eyes and a round face. It didn't matter to me that he wasn't my biological father. He was just my dad.

My father, Harry William, was an executive with the Uniroyal tire company, traveling by train to New York City daily. He had a presence about him, and at six feet, four inches, you couldn't miss him. He was smart, advised to go into law school after being a standout on his college debate team. My father was handsome, thoughtful, more serious than not, and a faithful, loving husband, as well as a great dad. I recall my dad stating, "Why would I want margarine when I have butter at home?" in reference to never going out with the guys after work. My father was a World War II veteran and flew C-47 sky train military transport planes. Dad didn't talk about the war much, but I do recall a story about him flying over the Himalayan mountains, which he referred to as "the hump." That's probably why I remember the story because all the other details elude me. I saw aerial photographs of Hiroshima dated six weeks after the bombing that were taken by scientists through the large cargo doors of the reconnaissance plane being flown by my father over the devastated area.

He loved the outdoors and everything that it has to offer. Family and family time was extremely important to him, I think, because number one, he was an only child, and number two, his dad died suddenly at age fifty-two of an apparent heart attack, two weeks after my dad turned twenty-one. He graduated from Hofstra University at age twenty-two but never did go on to law school. I'm sure his father's passing had something to do with that, but I really don't know. He loved having family meetings, usually after church but before Sunday dinner, during which we would talk about current events, things going on in school or sports, or many a time, he would just read poetry. Truth be told, growing up, this was just a huge pain in the ass.

My mother, Ruth Gwendolyn, was a stay-at-home mom, typical for the 1950s. She was pretty, with a slim figure, soft wavy brown hair, and generally small features with the exception of her nine and a half shoe size. Mom had a childlike enthusiasm of the world, often getting excited seeing a rainbow, hearing a favorite song on the radio, or her excitement while witnessing new flowers bloom in her gardens. It never ceased to amaze me how she found joy in the most mundane things. My mother was known as the Hallmark lady to friends and family alike, sending cards to say thank you or acknowledge a wedding, anniversary, birthdays, or just a quick hello. It truly gave her pleasure. She always decorated the house both inside and out on *every* holiday. There were plastic bins on shelves in our basement, each lined up and labeled with the appropriate holiday. One of my mother's favorite holidays was Halloween. She would get so excited when the doorbell rang with kids all dressed up, looking to fill their containers with candy, not expecting a grown woman answering the door with a Bozo the clown mask and a wicked sounding laugh. I am sure half the children in our neighborhood were scared to death. I never liked that mask, and that's probably why Halloween is my least favorite holiday. Mom was clearly the disciplinarian in our household but my dad could stop you in your tracks with just one look. It didn't happen often, but you just knew to let it go. My mother affectionately called me

Daisy while frequently lamenting "I hope you have six daughters just like you."

My mother could be irreverent at times. When we were a little older, say high school age, and each of us was asking her to do this or to help with that, she would turn to us and state with a smirk, "Well, why don't I stick a broom up my ass and sweep the floor as well."

Her demure stature did not match her ability to quiet a room. She was talkative, at times loud, a chatterbox some might say, with a deep, almost gravelly-sounding voice. She had an authoritative quality to speaking, which somehow made you listen, and Mom had the uncanny ability to talk about anything, everything, and nothing…to anyone.

Most nights, we would have dinner together as a family, no TV, just conversation. We each had our designated seats around this large mahogany table. Matching chairs were high backed with no arms and seats made of wicker. When my father walked in from the train station, promptly at 6:35, he said a quick hello to us and changed into more comfortable clothes. My mother would have his drink chilling in the refrigerator, always a Manhattan, then he would read the paper until dinner was called. Frequently, my dad would ask each of us what "interesting or productive" things we did that day, each being called upon and expected to contribute. Most nights were fun and lighthearted, while occasionally, others turned into more serious conversations like the one about bullying. Each of us usually made something up, which I'm sure they knew because all we wanted to do was finish dinner so we could go outside or get to the basement first so you had control of the small black-and-white TV clicker. Looking back, it was a very special time. Nevertheless, the decades of the sixties and seventies were like no other. The illusion of innocence of Americans as a society was starting to erode. There was Vietnam, the draft, the assassinations of John F. Kennedy, Robert F. Kennedy, and Martin Luther King. The nation watched its first moon landing and witnessed the civil rights movement, Cuban missile crisis, Kent State, passage of the Equal Rights Amendment, Woodstock, and Watergate. Sexual freedoms, drugs, and protests were the norm. It was one of those defining periods in American history that moved us forward or backward, depending on your view. I imagine it must have been an extremely difficult time to parent.

We lived in a three-bedroom ranch-style home with a one-car garage and a good-size backyard. We were not wealthy but comfortably middle class. Since I was the only girl, I got to have my own bedroom while my brothers shared a room with a half wall divider down the middle. I know neither of them really liked it, but there was no other choice. A six-year age difference was enormous, especially when Curt went into high school, and Gregg was only in the third grade. The only grand-parent I ever knew was my father's mother. She passed away when I was ten, but I do have fond memories of her. She was a larger than life character, literally and figuratively, being both tall and wide. Huge would be an appropriate description of my grandmother, standing over six feet tall and weighing well over three hundred pounds. Both of my mom's parents passed away within one year of each other when my parents were first married.

Each summer, we took a two-week vacation, camping in the Adirondack Mountains in upstate New York. I think that's where I developed a love of the outdoors. Just the smell of evergreen trees and campfires brings back wonderful memories.

I definitely was more of a tomboy than a girly girl, playing army more than with dolls. As the neighborhood boys outnumbered the girls, three to one, I just wanted to be included, much to the dismay of Curt. We were always outside if the weather was nice, playing some sort of game with all the other neighborhood kids—red light, green light, dodgeball, running bases, and my favorite—flashlight tag. It was totally normal to walk into any one of these neighbors' homes to use the bathroom or get a glass of water. All the kids had their own special signal from their parents to let them know it was time to get home. Ours was a boat horn, very loud and not easily missed. We spent many summer days with neighbors, gathering in the backyard, enjoying barbecues, putting on skits, talent shows, and concerts. As a child I didn't realize how fortunate my parents were to have lifelong friendships develop from that close-knit neighborhood. They frequently gathered for dinner parties or to play bridge at each other's houses. One evening I was awoken by loud music and singing. I snuck into the living room, giving me a perfect view of Aunt Jane being rolled up in our braided rug, then lifted up and pranced around the house. I call the few that are still with us aunts and uncles, and feel incredibly lucky to say that. To this day, I am blessed to have close contact with many of the kids from that wonderful neighborhood on Long Island.

Holidays were always spent with my mother's only other sibling, Aunt Ginny, and her husband, Uncle Jim, and my cousins Jill, Jimmy and Jean. They lived in the next town, just a short fifteen-minute drive.

I have great memories of spending time with my three cousins as holidays were always alternated between our homes, as well as occasionally taking family vacations together. The most memorable trip we took was when my dad and Uncle Jim rented a houseboat for all ten of us for two weeks in the US Virgin Islands. I was sixteen, a time when you really don't want to hang with your parents, but this trip was amazing. Bright sunny days spent repeatedly jumping off the bow of the boat and cool nights playing games on the upper deck. Warm summer breezes permeated the air with the smell of coconut and pineapple. By far, the bluest and most inviting water I had ever seen. The sun shining off the water looked magical with a beautiful turquoise hue as I learned how to snorkel while holding my breath and diving toward the bottom to inspect coral or schools of fish. My love for the sea was sealed that week.

I truly loved my high school years. I was an average student who stressed significantly about final exams and standardized tests, having interests much more social than academic. I guess the label fit. I was a cheerleader throughout my high school years as well as played field hockey and was a member of the modern dance troupe. I took a job in my sophomore year as a waitress at Howard Johnson's restaurant and enjoyed the job but especially loved the money. I still remember coming home after work and pouring all the nickels, dimes, quarters, and dollar bills out of the deep pockets from my HoJo uniform. My dad used to get such a kick out of that. Funny the things you remember. I enjoyed a large circle of friends from the neighborhood, church, and school. I think everyone sees their childhood through different lenses, and looking back, it was a time of innocence, of being carefree and loved.

Gregg, Dale, and Curt

Dale's ninth birthday

Family Portrait 1958   Harry in Pilot
Training WWII

Family Portrait 1970

Dale 1960

Dale, Curt, Grandma, Gregg and Dad

Defining Moments

I believe each of us has defining moments, memories that are etched in your brain and somehow define and shape who you are. One of those moments for me came during a summer camping trip in the Adirondack Mountains with my family. One particular night, the campground was hosting a social with a couple of local bands in the big rec hall located at the entrance of this large and densely forested campground. In the fall, I would be going into middle school, having just turned thirteen, and was really looking forward to this battle of the bands. My parents got me a portable turntable for my birthday with a pouch on the inside cover to hold my 45s and the lid with lock and key was painted black with a tiny circle in the center to resemble an album. I loved it and spent many hours listening to Barbra Streisand songs and the musical Oklahoma while singing into my hairbrush. Music was always a centerpiece in our home. I was incredibly fortunate to see the Beatles at Forest Hills Tennis Stadium in 1964. My dad, mom, Curt, and I watched them land in a helicopter and perform among a sea of screaming people. It was thrilling, mesmerizing, and deafening.

Walking up to the hall, I remember it being extremely loud and crowded. I made my way over to one corner of this large log cabin-style room, leaning against a round wooden pole, trying to avoid my little brother. A slow song started to play, and I saw this cute guy walk across the floor directly toward me. I immediately straightened up and put my glasses on top of my head. I have amblyopia or lazy eye and have been wearing glasses since I was six years old. Not sure why, but at that moment, I took them off quickly and realized I didn't have any pockets, so I just put them on top of my head. And with that, this guy walked up to me and asked if I would like to dance. I said sure and followed him a few steps to the dance floor, putting both of my hands on his shoulders as he put his hands around my waist. We swayed back and forth, not saying a word until the song ended, and he gently took my hand and walked me back to that pole. He said "thank you for the dance," while turning to walk away as I was unable to utter a word. That was my first dance with a boy, as well as the last time I ever wore my glasses in public.

On a different kind of defining moment, I was in tenth grade, fifteen years old and just starting to date a boy named Scott. He was tall and skinny with a full head of curly brown hair, a junior in high school, and I thought completely adorable. Dating meant getting together in groups at school or with friends at someone's home. I never actually went on a real date with Scott, but we always hung out together. Over our school Christmas break, the back doorbell rang and I was hoping it was Bob, Jeff, and Connie as we had made tentative plans to play cards that evening. Instead, I saw Scott with his big toothy smile, curly hair sticking out of his knitted winter hat standing there holding a wrapped Christmas present, as my heart raced a little. I quickly opened the door as a gusty wind blew so he could step in and get out of the freezing cold. I introduced him to my parents, who had never met him before, and we proceeded to our finished basement as I definitely knew my father would never have wanted me to bring Scott to my bedroom. I also remember being embarrassed as I did not have a present for him but proceeded to our basement and opened his gift. It was a bottle of Jean Nate cologne in that distinctive yellow and black package. It smelled divine.

Sometime in mid-January, I had just arrived at school and headed to my first class, which was algebra. A friend of mine ran up to me clearly upset with tears in her eyes and barely able to get the words out that Scott had been killed by a hit-and-run driver the night before while walking home after a basketball game. I found myself outside in the bleachers opposite the field house, sobbing uncontrollably. The next thing I recall, my math teacher was sitting next to me as I tried unsuccessfully to keep it together. I thought he was going to be angry that I ran out of his class, but actually, he just hugged me, and after calming down, he persuaded me to get back into school before I froze to death. I later found out that he had already known about Scott and was worried about me when I ran out of class. He knew we were friends. At this point in my life, I had only known one other person to die, and that was my grandmother. This seemed so absurd and unbelievable. How could somebody so young be dead? Mr. Spada made a lasting impression as I saw for the first time a teacher as a compassionate human being with emotions and feelings like everyone else. Up until that very moment, teachers were just another adult telling me what to do. I realized then the loss of Scott profoundly affected our school and community as a whole. Three years later, as graduation from high school was approaching, I wrote that math teacher a note acknowledging his impact on my life and expressing my gratitude for his compassion during that difficult time. To this very day, some fifty years later, I can't stand the smell of Jean Nate.

Dale: Spring of 1972

High school graduation was fast approaching, and I needed to figure out what I wanted to do with my life. Looking back now at age eighteen, I was quite immature and naive. I believe our parents wrapped us in a cocoon trying to protect us from realities and the darker sides of life. I'm not sure that was the right thing to do, but it was obviously the way they chose to parent. So off I went to a two-year all-girl junior college in Massachusetts that enrolled less than three hundred students, a huge difference from my high school which consisted of over nine hundred students in just my graduating class. I was definitely looking for a smaller, more intimate setting, and I was hoping to have found it at Lasell Junior College. My thoughts were that I would transfer after two years and acquire a bachelor's degree in early childhood education. By starting out at a junior college, it enabled me the option of changing my mind on a major, which was very undecided, as I would have two years and most of the required courses completed.

Many of the dorms on campus were big beautiful mansions with the exception of one large ugly cement block dorm. I was fortunate to have been placed in one of those large stately homes with big rooms shared by two or three girls and one bathroom on each of the three floors. There were high ceilings, nonworking beautiful fireplaces, and mahogany staircases. I thought it was elegant, and just loved it. I looked forward to the camaraderie with all the girls, something I envisioned as a huge sleepover party with some classes thrown in. I did make some wonderful lifelong friendships, but I was not prepared for all the secrets, backstabbing, crying, and plain old drama that some of those girls thrived on.

Freshman year my roommate was a girl named Jackie from Buffalo, New York. I thought she was so pretty, spunky, and exuded confidence. Jackie was tiny, maybe one hundred pounds soaking wet, and not more than five feet tall and told me that she buys her blue jeans in the boy's department because they fit the best. She said it in a strange way, and I was never quite sure if that embarrassed her. The next day after settling in and each making our little space our own, Jackie said that she needed my help. She thought she was able to handle this herself but couldn't manage, and I said, "Sure, how can I help?"

She lifted up her shirt, undid her bra, pulled it up, and stated, "I need your help pulling these coarse, wiry sutures out of both my breasts from having breast reduction surgery three weeks prior."

I wasn't expecting that the first week I met her, and I truly had no idea you could reduce your breast size.

One embarrassing situation happened while hitchhiking with a girlfriend into Boston for a night out. We often hitchhiked in the seventies but never alone. An old beat-up Chevy pulled over and offered us a ride. I remember the back seat being filled with junk, boxes on top of boxes, and a guitar case with a music stand draped over. Both Leslie and I got in the front seat, me getting in first, her second, by the door, as we were kind of squished together. The young man driving asked if either of us wanted to play his instrument, and I proceeded to say, "What instrument do you play?" as Leslie not so subtly started elbowing me in the ribs, saying, "This is fine. We will get out here." At times, I felt out of place and awkward while everyone else seemed so worldly.

Another one of those crossroads in life happened at Christmas time of 1973 while I was trying to fly to Michigan for the first time as my parents literally moved from Long Island, New York, three weeks earlier. The airline had overbooked my flight, a common practice in the seventies, and subsequently, I was unable to get on any flight that afternoon. I finally found an empty phone booth at the airport and called my parents, who were quite annoyed thinking I missed my flight but finally understood the predicament I was in. I was rebooked on a flight leaving the next day, but that didn't really help my current situation as Lasell was closed for the holiday break. I knew I could get into my room, but there wasn't going to be one other person in that big house. So, I hopped in a cab and headed to my favorite bar on Beacon Street in Boston called Fathers Two. This was a frequent hangout, and I knew I would recognize quite a few people. As I exited the taxi directly across the street in a vacant lot, gathered my suitcase and purse, I noticed Frank walking down the street toward the bar. We had only known each other for a short amount of time, barely a month, but I was beginning to have feelings for him. He seemed fun and cool with his blue jean jacket and long hair. I shouted his name as he came running over and kissed me before I even got to finish my airport saga story. I finally made it to Michigan that cold, windy December day, arriving at Detroit airport on time, but my heart was in Boston.

My parents moved to Bloomfield Hills, Michigan, six months before I was to graduate college as my dad got a promotion to run the tire division for Uniroyal's Midwest operations. It was a job he was very much looking forward to. So Mom packed up everything after living in the same home and raising three kids for more than twenty-five years. They purchased a big four-bedroom home in a family-friendly neighborhood with a two-car garage and a large flat backyard, all surrounded by beautiful landscaping. My older brother had already graduated from college and was living in Florida with his girlfriend, soon to be wife. My younger brother was just starting his sophomore year in high school. It was a difficult time for any adolescent to switch schools, but Gregg was an athlete and managed to make some friends early on. In 1973, I spent my first Christmas in our new home in Michigan. It was big and lovely, but it wasn't home to me, and I couldn't wait to get back to school, if only for the last semester before graduation.

Dale: Spring 1974

As my final days at Lasell were fast approaching, with an associate's degree in early childhood education in hand and the intention to get my bachelor's degree in the near future, I saw a clearer vision and a more appropriate understanding of this world—the good, the bad, and the ugly.

I knew my parents would be driving to Boston in less than a week in our new station wagon to bring home all the stuff I had accumulated over the last two years. Now I needed to figure out my next step. My roommate and I decided to get an apartment together in Boston and find jobs. I thought it was a perfect plan as Michigan was never an option for me, but *everything* came to a screeching halt after being home exactly one week. My father, having just turned fifty-two years old, dropped dead in the bleachers during Gregg's high school baseball game while he was pitching. I literally, that day, started working at Howard Johnson's.

On this late Thursday afternoon in May 1974, life as I had known it was never going to be the same. A neighbor whom I did not know came into Howard Johnson's, introduced himself to me, and stated that my father had collapsed during a baseball game and was taken to the hospital by ambulance, but that was all they knew. They volunteered to pick me up and bring me to the hospital. I remember being nervous and scared, my heart suddenly pounding. Nobody talked very much on the way, except I recall the women saying they were sorry they didn't have any more information. Upon arriving, I was escorted into a typical-looking waiting room where I spotted my mother and brother sitting in the back, facing each other. I knew right away that my dad was gone. Apparently, he had suffered a massive heart attack and arrived at the hospital DOA. We hugged and cried, but it didn't seem real to me. How could my father, who I talked to four hours ago, be gone?

I have hazy memories of the ride back home with the exception of being in someone's car whom I did not know. Shortly after arriving home, Gregg's baseball coach, who was also his high school science teacher, drove my parents' car to our house and was followed by his wife in their car. There were lots of hugs and "I'm so sorry for your loss." I remember not being able to cry that night and wondering why. I was probably in shock.

My father knew of and consented to my plans of moving back to Boston but insisted on me having a minimum of $800 in the bank before I could leave. That's why I got the job at Howard Johnson's. Now everything was thrown up in the air, and I didn't know where all the pieces were going to land.

Curt, Aunt Ginny, and Uncle Jim flew out the next morning to help with the arrangements and to be together. What was going to happen? How would we all manage without him? Would my mother keep this house after just six months or move back to Long Island? So many unanswered questions. It was such an unbelievable sudden loss. It was so hard to comprehend, and I found it difficult to sleep that first night. When I got up to get some water, while still dark outside, I saw my mother in her bedroom ironing what looked like dish towels. It was not a usual thing for her to do, and she was kind of mumbling to no one. I couldn't imagine what she was going through. Everything was happening so fast—no time for getting things in order and certainly no goodbyes. My father was the love of my mother's life, and that love was blown apart in an instant.

I spent the next four months that awful summer in Michigan because I just couldn't leave her. She was a mess. At age fifty-one, my mom was widowed and living in a new place with no family nearby, except Gregg and I. I can't imagine her fear, hurt, and loneliness.

The neighbors were incredibly supportive throughout the next couple of weeks, which truly were a blur.

Meals kept arriving. Flowers and cards seemed to be everywhere. I detested all the arrangements in every room and the way my Mom displayed all the cards. I didn't want them. I just wanted my dad back. I hated all the nameless people ringing our doorbell with condolences as my mom was more than gracious, and I didn't understand her behavior. Everybody handles grief differently, and I apparently wanted to shut everybody out. It took me a long time to understand that friends, neighbors, and my father's coworkers needed to do these things as a way for them to grieve.

I spent most of my time that summer working and socializing with the few friends I made from Howard Johnson's. My mom remembered my father's directive for me to have at least $800 in the bank before I could move, and she was sticking to it. I worked as many hours as I could and life slowly began to return to some normalcy, for me anyway. I desperately missed my dad, but work and friends and my goal of moving to Boston to be with Frank helped me through this terrible summer. I do not have many regrets in my life, but the most difficult was never getting to know my father as an adult. I truly feel cheated. He passed away the week before my twentieth birthday as we were just beginning to acknowledge that subtle change when your child becomes an adult—more introspective conversations and a certain kind of respect. It was palpable to me and then taken away so quickly.

I don't think my mom was ever quite the same again. She was only fifty-one when he passed and never dated anyone even though she lived until she was ninety-one.

Connie, Dale, Jeff, and Bobby from the neighborhood

Harry, Dale, and Ruth. College Graduation 1974

Frank and Dale, 1975

Ruth and Harry

Harry and Ruth 1943

Dale: Fall of 1974...Moving On

My college friend had obviously moved on, and Frank and I had been dating, albeit long distance, so our plan was for me to move back to Boston and get an apartment together. I know that sounds crazy as we were so young, having just turned twenty and Frank twenty-one. As Ed Sheeran wrote, "We were just kids when we fell in love." It was hard leaving my mother, and I felt guilty, but was feeling somewhat stifled living at home after being on my own for two years. I knew that if I didn't leave Michigan soon, I would never be able to. I moved in with Frank on September 26, 1974, four months to the day after my dad passed, on a crisp fall day with the most brilliant sky, into a rather dumpy apartment in Boston near Cleveland Circle. It desperately needed some TLC. It was a fifth-floor walk-up with one good-size bedroom, a small but functional bathroom, an alley kitchen opened to a bright living room and located directly across the street from a Massachusetts Bay Transit Authority station, better known as the T.

I used that green line T station to get into Boston daily at my new job at Chilton corporation, a credit reporting firm. My job as a customer service representative consisted of mostly women in a large room all sitting at a desk with a computer and each wearing a bulky headset. We were waiting for incoming calls from banks, retailers, and credit unions checking on individuals requesting a loan or credit card. After several years, I became a supervisor and then a corporate trainer. I traveled mostly throughout New England to various credit reporting agencies to train new hires or conduct seminars on updates. I loved the small group seminars as well as the one-on-ones. However, the larger attended seminars, with upward of a hundred people, were infrequent but no less terrifying to me as I never quite got comfortable speaking in front of large groups. I always felt like a deer in the headlights with a squeaky high-pitched voice. I was once told I sounded like Tiny Tim and looked as if I might pass out. I never did and somehow always managed to get through it. When not traveling, I was responsible for the major banks and retailers in downtown Boston. I did love getting dressed up each day, always carrying a briefcase stuffed with supplies and updates. I knew where every pay phone was located, no cell phones then, as well as all the good ladies' rooms. Life was pretty damn good in Boston with a great partner, a good job, and some money in our pockets.

Three years later, on a cool fall day on the first of October 1977, Frank and I were the first of our friends to get married. We were wed in the Syosset Community Church, in Syosset, New York on Long Island, where I was baptized and spent many Sunday mornings throughout my childhood. As I approached the tall heavy white oak doors, I quietly reflected on how many times I had gone through those doors with my dad. I just knew he was watching down on all of us this day. It had only been three years since my father's passing, and I know it was difficult for my mother on many levels. The fact that she lived in Michigan, I lived in Boston, and the wedding was taking place in New York didn't make it any easier. I wore my mother's wedding dress after her gentle persuasion and had both my brothers walk me down the aisle.

Mom and I never had a constructive conversation about finances for the wedding. I was young, not really an excuse, but was apprehensive to have a meaningful wedding budget discussion. As a family, we never talked much about money, budgets or finances but after my father passed away my mother was even more closed off. At times, Mom could be frugal and her reluctance to talk about money made this upcoming wedding difficult to plan. Her main focus was the venue and the menu. Things like flowers, invitations, photography, and everything else that goes into a wedding, she left up to me. I kept track of everything as she would send me a check to cover the costs. Having just a little savings, Frank and I tried to cut costs where we thought we could. Bobby, my dear childhood friend, graciously agreed to be the photographer. Looking back, it was really unfair of me to have my friend shoulder the total responsibility for all our wedding photos. Some sixty years later we are still close, and as the song goes, "You can't make old friends." We had a lovely reception with about a hundred people at the Huntington Yacht Club with much-appreciated help from Aunt Ginny, who lived in Huntington. Everyone mingled while taking in the beautiful views of Long Island Sound during the cocktail hour. We honeymooned in St. Thomas, Virgin Islands, and after two gorgeous, warm days, a tropical storm approached and dumped over ten inches of rain as the National Guard was called in for fear of mudslides. Not really how I envisioned my honeymoon.

We bought our first home in 1984 in a town thirty minutes north of Boston called Andover. The neighborhood was reminiscent of my own childhood, with lots of young adults raising children.

I always knew I wanted to be a mother. It was never a question. It was merely a fact that was going to happen to me in my lifetime. But sometimes, life throws you curveballs. We had been married for over four years and decided to start a family, and after a year of trying with no success, we went to a fertility specialist. Over the next several years, we endured all kinds of treatments, tests, and procedures. I recall before one of many such appointments, Frank and I met at a hotel bar off RT 128 in Newton where I handed him a sealed specimen jar into which he deposited a "sample". I immediately put in between my breasts to keep warm, as I was instructed to do, and drove to the fertility office three miles away. After being inseminated, I sat there with two pillows under my butt with my legs straight up in the air for about thirty minutes. It was a difficult time both physically and mentally as well as a financial strain, but we never gave up hope, and somehow deep down, I knew I was going to be a mother. One way or another, either through IVF, a new procedure, insemination, a natural pregnancy, or adoption, I was determined.

I then discovered I was pregnant after Frank and I returned home from a two-week vacation to England and France in the summer of 1985. The clinic called it a "spontaneous pregnancy" as it did not involve any of the treatments or procedures we had endured over the last five years. Sitting in the doctor's office I felt tired and kind of fuzzy, chalking it up to being jet lagged. Somewhere, deep down I knew I was pregnant, even before taking the test that revealed it to be true. Panic set in quickly realizing that I drank wine every day over the course of those two weeks. The doctor said something like not to worry, it was probably why I got pregnant in the first place and then stated that it was too early in the pregnancy to do any real harm. At the age of thirty-one, I delivered our miracle baby boy, who we named Alexander Francis on March 27, 1986. For the first time in my life, I had a genetic connection. I remember looking at him, thinking who does he resembles, where is that adorable pug nose from, and those beautiful pink lips. It was beyond amazing. I was finally a mom. I vividly recall the warm breezy day we brought Alex home and placed him on the coffee table still in his car seat, turning to Frank and saying, "What do we do now?"

Frank, looking a little shocked, said, "I can't believe they let us out of the hospital with him."

Dale and Frank's Wedding

Curt, Mom, and Gregg (circa 1987)

Dale and Frank (Summer of 1985)

Bob and Dale

Frank and Alex (Newborn)

Frank, Dale and Alex (Age Nine Months)

Ann: Moving on—Fall of 1956

Returning home after my stay with Uncle Larry and Aunt Nannie, I was anxious to move on and took a temporary job at Saint Stephen's Episcopal Church in Olean, helping in the office. There was not much work, and honestly, I was quite bored, but at least it kept me somewhat occupied and out of the house. I wanted to go back to Katherine Gibbs in the worst way, but I just couldn't bring myself to follow through with all that entailed. I had left so abruptly and never stayed in contact with any of the girls, and I'm sure I was the topic of much gossip as it was pretty obvious when I left that I was pregnant. A month after returning, I received a call from one of my sorority sisters who was living in Philadelphia and looking for someone to share her apartment. I jumped at the chance, and my parents were equally glad that I was finally moving on and frankly, I believe, finally moving out. I needed to forge ahead and stop dwelling in the past year. It was just that, in the past, behind me, no regrets and time to start moving forward and living my life.

So I packed up and moved to Philly, and after getting settled, my first priority was to get an appointment with an employment agency and start looking for a job. My sorority sister started working at a school for the blind and put me in touch with the same employment agency that helped her. After several interviews, which included a typing and dictation test, I was hired as a secretary at a small public relations firm located in downtown Philadelphia. It was mildly fun, and I quickly began learning how to fit in with this small but professional team. My months at Katie Gibbs had paid off as I was proficient with all the equipment that made this public relations firm run smoothly. I felt like I was making a real contribution as well as learning a lot about this unique business. I was finally living and working on my own, and it was such an incredible feeling.

I had been working for about eight months when I met Bill. He worked in an office several floors down from where I worked, and we began talking in the elevator daily. I thought he was good-looking with a sophisticated manner, and he finally asked if I'd like to go out for drinks sometime after work. We met at a bar around the corner from our building and found a quiet corner where we shared stories and enjoyed cocktails. We continued getting together after work at least once a week, which was a wonderful way to get to know each other.

One particular day, Bill seemed not quite himself, distant and morose. This was less than a month after we started seeing each other, and I couldn't imagine what had him so down. He finally told me that he was in the process of going through a divorce. I was shocked and confused and frankly really pissed. We had only been dating for a short time, and I was flattered by all his attention but could never have continued the relationship if I thought I was the cause of the demise of his marriage. He steadfastly promised the marriage had ended well before I met him and had been waiting for just the right time to tell me. The divorce was taking much longer than Bill anticipated with financial demands, custody concerns, and breaking up of a household. That's when he told me about his two children, a son and daughter, both elementary school age. They lived with their mother, but he saw them frequently, making sure each was comfortable and had their own room in his apartment. They had been separated and living apart for well over a year but insisted he had a good relationship with both of his children.

Surprisingly, none of that scared me off. At this very early stage in our relationship, we both concede that we had to be honest and truthful not only about our past lives but also moving forward if we were ever going to succeed as a couple. So I confided in him about the baby girl I gave up two years prior. He accepted the existence of my biological child gracefully, and it was never discussed again. I guess I had fallen for him more than I realized but needed to think about what was best for me. I decided to move to Boston as my roommate was getting ready to be married, and another friend that I had met in Philadelphia was going to Boston. It sounded like great fun with more job opportunities. I think deep down, I was also trying to figure out if Bill and I were truly meant to be. I'm not sure why I thought the distance would help, but I moved to Boston in the fall of 1956. Jeannie and I found a small two-bedroom, one-bathroom apartment on Marlboro Street, a quiet tree-lined section in the Back Bay of Boston.

It took me less than two weeks to be hired as a secretary in a lab at Massachusetts General Hospital doing research on isotopes. It was great fun, and the training to do this specific lab work was challenging and fascinating and something I discovered I loved. I saw Bill almost every weekend as he would take the train from Philly to Boston, eagerly looking forward to Friday when I got to see him again. It was such a wonderful time in my life as I had a job I loved and a man that truly loved and cared about me.

We dated long distance for a little over a year, and in the late fall of 1957, we decided to marry. My parents were elated, and a wedding date was set for September 20, 1958.

We had a small wedding at our local church in Olean, New York. It turned out to be a spectacular day after a morning of rain and fog. It was relatively warm for a late September day, and I remember how perfect everything felt. My father walked me down the aisle, and as I turned to hug him, I saw tears in his eyes. My dad wasn't exceptionally emotional, usually being the calm, cool, collected guy, so this behavior was not typical, and I quickly turned and grabbed Bill's hand. At the reception, I remember my father getting up and giving the most eloquent toast, and it was my turn to have tears in my eyes.

We honeymooned on a trip to the West Coast for ten glorious days. We drove along the magnificent Pacific coastline, stopping at quaint inns along the way. Bill was in the process of relocating his business to the New York area, so we settled into a one-bedroom apartment in Manhattan on East End Avenue across from a beautiful park with lots of areas for children of all ages to play.

Michael arrived in the summer of 1959 and I stopped working so I could be home full time with my new baby.

Many hours were spent at the park across the street meeting interesting women with young children like my own. During the early months, pregnant with our second child, I received a phone call nobody is ever prepared for. My mom was calling to let me know that my dad had died. Through a shaky but somehow steady voice, I learned he had an aneurysm in his chest, was rushed to the hospital to be operated on, but the surgeons found his arteries and veins were too damaged from high blood pressure to have any kind of a successful outcome. He died that afternoon. It was all very sudden, with little to no warning.

My mother was only fifty-seven years old when he died that spring of 1961. She seemed to adjust to being a widow pretty well, but then, my mother was always a private person. She would visit us often, enjoying all the galleries and museums in New York as well as spending time with Michael. A few months before Polly arrived, Mom and I took a mini vacation to Florence, Italy, exploring all the famous and not so famous galleries. She continued to live in the house on Madison Avenue, where I grew up, never once contemplating moving to a smaller place. This is where she raised her family, and this is where she wanted to stay. Many summers, Michael and Polly, along with Jim's three oldest daughters, would all go to Mary's house for a week. She must have been exhausted but never complained. All the grandkids loved it because she let them do whatever they wanted. Mary lived a long, fulfilling, but somewhat lonely life until she died in 1998 at the age of ninety-seven.

When Polly came along in 1962, Bill and I decided to search for a larger apartment. I so enjoyed life in the city that moving to the suburbs to a large house with a white picket fence never appealed to me. Each summer, while the kids were out of school, we stayed on our houseboat, called "The Garnet" in the Hamptons on the tip of Long Island, New York. I loved the city, but it was a wonderful distraction from all the hustle and bustle. Unbeknownst to me, Bill had been researching property to purchase in North River, New York, in the Adirondacks ever since a fishing trip with some buddies. We purchased a section of undeveloped land and began the process of converting it to a ski area, always a dream of Bill's. We named it Harvey Mountain after the mountain it sat on and had it cleared, cut trails, and put in a T-bar. We spent every weekend that summer working on getting ready for ski season. There was a large stone house on the property where we stayed, and we opened our first season at Christmas time of 1962 to the delight of both our families and the public who came in droves.

We operated on weekends only for the next seventeen years, commuting back to New York City each Sunday evening and returning on Friday afternoons. At times, it was stressful, running a business and all the commuting, but Bill's business, which was recruiting for executive job placement, was taking off and paying the bills.

As the children's educational needs developed, we found a private boys' school in Manhattan for Michael called Trinity and when Polly was ready for school, we entered her into the sister school called Nightingale.

Both kids thrived early and developed many wonderful friendships. However, it became apparent that both Michael and Polly suffer from dyslexia, and as time went on, school became much more difficult for both of them. The private schools offered many wonderful opportunities, but teaching children with any kind of disability was not on their radar. Structure and procedures to think outside the box and help children with dyslexia or any learning disability was a fight we were not going to win with the administration of either school. So when Michael was fourteen and Polly just turning twelve, we decided to move to Glens Falls, New York. It was a community near Lake George and just north of Saratoga Springs. We had researched the school system, and it seemed like a good fit, plus it was very close to Harvey Mountain. We settled in as Bill continued to work in the city, taking the train early Tuesday mornings and returning Friday afternoon.

The public schools in Glens Falls were much better suited for both our children with clearer communication, cooperation, and understanding about dyslexia from the administration than we got at the private schools. It was a struggle at first for both of them but something that each adapted to in their own way. As it turned out, we discovered Bill has dyslexia as well and learned it is a familial disability and can be passed down from generation to generation. He struggled greatly in high school and college, but at that time, there was no recognition or help for anyone afflicted with dyslexia.

Life was moving along quickly as it seems to do so often. I definitely missed city life and all the things you could do right outside your door, but I was adjusting to life in the country. The kids were involved in many after school activities as well as skiing as often as permitted. Both had become expert skiers by high school and spent more time at Gore Mountain than our Harvey Mountain, which became too tame for each of them. As the children grew older, I became more involved in community affairs and volunteered at a local hospital, a local library, and the historical museum in nearby Albany. I started playing tennis and enjoyed bridge, although I was nowhere near as skilled as my mother.

Both children finished high school in Glens Falls, New York, and went out west to Utah to ski as well as complete their college degrees. Polly and Michael both met their future spouses and settled into life in Utah. Both were passionate about skiing, and Polly made this her career. To date, she still teaches and guides skiers at Deer Valley in Park City, Utah.

Sometime around 1975, the Adirondack Park agency came into existence and developed strict rules for those of us who owned land in the newly formed park. They zoned our area so we could not expand the trails nor build any houses on the property, which had been our long-range plan. This made signage and directions to Harvey Mountain almost impossible as nobody could find us. We changed the name to Garnet mountain to indicate it was on the Garnet Mine Road in North River, trying to outfox the state and their new rules. In the end, after several long years, they finally wore us down, and Bill decided to sell to the state of New York. They paid us $90,000 and agreed to have the land go back to "forever wild" status, which is where it is today.

They were good years, if a lot of work. Bill retired and closed his company E. A. Butler Associates when he reached sixty-five. We bought an RV and did some traveling and then bought a larger one and settled in an RV park in Naples, Florida. We sold the RV after only two years and purchased a condo in Eagle Creek, a community within Naples. We spent many a winter there, playing golf, tennis, and bridge before Bill died in 2007 after a short illness. I kept Eagle Creek for several more years but finally sold it in 2012 and settled into life as a widow back in Glens Falls, New York. Several years have passed, and it was becoming more apparent I needed surgery on my lower back to relieve spasms that made walking and standing for any length of time difficult, and I opted for the procedure at Massachusetts General Hospital.

It was about this time that two grand surprises came into my life.

Harvey Mountain Skiers

Harvey Mountain

Ann (circa 2008)

Ann and Bill

Dale: Winter of 2001

Mom was really starting to show signs of dementia. She was still living in the same home she and Dad purchased in Michigan some thirty years earlier, and virtually, nothing had changed—same furniture, same pictures on the wall, same wallpaper in the bathroom, and the same drapery in the living room. It was as if time literally stopped so very long ago. After my dad died, Mom decided to remain in Michigan and start her new life as a widow. It surprised me she didn't pack up and move back to New York but instead told me she thought it was God's plan for her to stay in this home, in this new place and felt like returning to Long Island would be going backward.

Now at age eighty, she was still working in the local high school at a youth employment office after more than twenty-five years. Mom enthusiastically embraced her job, which was to coordinate outside employment opportunities with students looking for part-time work—everything from babysitting, lawn services, tutoring, and local restaurants in need of help.

She was passionate about her job and, as I've been told, the students loved her, often referring to her as Mama R. This petite woman, now less than five feet (having lost six inches in height from osteoporosis), with her deep gravelly voice, always had a line of students out the door. She loved talking to each and every one of them—empathy for some, ribbing for others. She always said you could tell "who was brought up properly" by how they acted around adults.

At the same time, as I was trying to get in touch with the high school principal to discuss an exit plan, she was trying to get in touch with me regarding my mom's noticeable inability to be effective at work any longer. It was becoming very apparent to all that Mom was having difficulty remembering simple tasks and would occasionally look at you with this blank stare. Gregg was living with her again, and initially, I felt better that somebody was watching out for her until it became apparent to me that he was only thinking of himself, and I neglectfully didn't realize how much he was drinking. His needs and desires were paramount while everything else became secondary, including mom. He was starting to spiral out of control with alcohol and drugs at the same time our mother was spiraling into her own out of control world. Both were desperately trying to hide what was going on.

Gregg's Journey

My brother Gregg had an adult life of much turmoil, self-doubt, and addiction. He was married and divorced twice, and each of those marriages produced one child. He was contacted by a biological half-sister after a four-plus-year search by her to locate him. His birth mother was not well, complications from lupus, when Gregg's siblings found him about fifteen years ago. His birth mother had five children with three different men, and most lived in and around the Rochester, New York area. This sister found a locket with some hair and questioned her mother as to whose baby hair it belonged to and was fully expecting it to be that of her younger brother, who was accidentally killed while cleaning a gun in his late teens. Kay, Gregg's birth mother, told her daughter it was her firstborn child whom she named Michael but gave up and placed in an adoption agency in New York City as an infant. She was either unwilling or unable to give her daughter any further details. After a total of four long years and an exhausting search before any Ancestry.com or 23andMe existed, she found Gregg while he was living in Michigan with Mom. He met Kay once after traveling to Rochester, New York, to meet his newfound family, but she was not well and wasn't able to answer any of Gregg's questions regarding his biological father, except that he lived in Florida. They kept in touch for a little while, but after his birth mother passed away, I think distance and differences made it easier for the relationships to fade.

Gregg was always a very good athlete with a natural hand to eye coordination. He pitched in the Little League World Series in Williamsport, Pennsylvania, at the age of eleven, and also played in the all-American amateur baseball tournament which started in 1945 and is still played each spring in Johnstown, Pennsylvania. Players ages seventeen to nineteen throughout the United States were invited to play by their high school or college coaches. Baseball was actually what got him through his junior and senior high school years after our dad passed away. He was a lefty pitcher, throwing 90 mph fastballs in high school. Many colleges were becoming interested, and I know this was a struggle for him as our father would have really helped him on this journey. My dad was always so supportive of Gregg and his athletic abilities, frequently attending games and encouraging him to keep practicing his skills. The age of sixteen is a hard enough time in a young man's life, let alone having just lost their dad—not quite a child anymore and not yet an adult. Gregg continued to play baseball in his remaining high school years and was eventually recruited and given a full baseball scholarship to Clemson University. Unfortunately, that's where the fairy tale ended, and a life of drugs and alcohol began. He was kicked out of school after freshman year for allegedly not having enough required courses to meet the standard for scholarships. Who knows what really happened? Always so much bullshit.

Over the next twenty-five years, Gregg had many jobs, mostly in sales that always ended with something that the company did or didn't do. It was never his fault. Addiction is such a debilitating disease, and I have come to believe that many alcoholics deceive themselves in the same way. It is just my opinion, but I find addictions and all that encompasses make some incredibly self-centered, always focusing on oneself. Whether it be at a time of using, life becomes a vicious cycle of lying, cheating, hiding, and stealing or recovery when you become more reflective and self-focused. I know that's going to piss some people off, but it has just been my experience. Some people figure it out while others have to hit rock bottom as they say in order to have a wake-up call to change. Some never get it. When alcohol and drugs become a *need,* not just a *want,* that's when it becomes dangerous. Addiction doesn't discriminate, rich or poor, educated or unschooled, family support or opposition—it impacts all.

Mom and I had many conversations about Gregg's behavior, but she was unable to do what he needed most, which was to boot his butt out of the house, stop enabling him, and picking up all his pieces.

As my mother was nearing her eightieth birthday, the signs of her forgetfulness were something we could no longer ignore. Her physical appearance was slightly off, having maybe an unmatched blouse or pants, but nothing too noticeable. She still kept herself put together with her hair always done and lipstick on. Her home was looking dirty, in need of a complete and thorough cleaning from top to bottom. Paper bags started to take over her bedroom, overflowing with mail, magazines and newspapers. It all overwhelmed me. Nothing was ever thrown out and Mom made it abundantly clear to not touch anything. "I know where everything is and will take care of it later." She was getting confused and frustrated about time, dates, and simple tasks seemed consuming at times.

Over the next several months, it became apparent that she needed additional help, way more than Gregg could have or should have handled. For her safety and well-being, I started researching assisted living facilities with a memory care unit. Curt, Gregg, and I agreed to have her come to Massachusetts so that she could be closer to me. After we moved Mom to Massachusetts and sold her home, Gregg decided to move to Florida. My gut reaction was that the environment would not be a good place for him with the warm Florida weather, beach bars, and a carefree lifestyle. Unknowingly at the time, this move would find him in a bad way, homeless, and more despondent than he could ever imagine *and* connect with someone that would forever change his life.

Over the next several years, I would get panicked phone calls that he didn't have any money for rent or food. I would send him cash and beg him to get some help. He said he was doing fine, just having a little bad luck. It was *always* some sort of excuse. As my mother declined, so did Gregg. His life was unraveling, and I was unable to trust him on any level. Phone calls became less and less, and weeks and months passed with little contact. He lost his job and his apartment, and I later found out he was living in his car. I recall one phone conversation so heart-wrenching as he gave me a vivid description of how he was beaten up the night before somewhere in a beach parking lot, apparently a homeless turf thing. They stole the little money he had and was asking for a "little help." I know I shouldn't have but again sent him a little money. He was spiraling out of control, and I truly didn't know what to do or how to help him, but I've since learned that there is nothing I could have done. He had to get sober on his own accord or it was never going to work. It had to come from him.

I had not talked to him in a couple of months and was getting worried as his only form of communication came from a prepaid phone, the kind purchased at a convenience store for a designated dollar amount. I didn't know whether he still had that phone as it always went to a generic voice mail. Finally, on this late fall afternoon, he called me to let me know that he was in an alcohol rehabilitation center in Titusville, Florida. He told me he sold his car to score some cocaine and vodka and spent the weekend with so-called friends, and after the drugs and alcohol were gone, he was literally kicked out. Gregg reluctantly, nervously, told me how he was walking down the street, feeling like he might throw up but just trying to figure out how to end this nightmare. He was "too chicken," his words, to jump off a bridge or stand in front of a train. He literally walked by a big red brick building that said, "Alcohol rehabilitation center," on the side facing the street in white spray paint. He walked in and was asked by someone at the desk if he really wanted help. He said yes and moved in that night, calling me several days later to let me know where he was. He was not doing well physically as the withdrawals from the cocaine and booze were severe. He was claiming to be nauseous, weak, and feeling like the worst flu he ever had. He sounded awful, but at least I knew Gregg was in a safe place with other people around if anything went wrong.

Months went by, and he seemed to be on the right track—not drinking or using. He was attending AA meetings daily, required to keep his room clean, do house chores, and prepare dinner with other residents each evening, followed by another meeting. Each day revolved around discussions of sobriety, behaviors, and attitudes, as well as a spiritual component, something he very much needed. The rehabilitation center that he walked into that day had been around for many years and helped thousands of people.

Rusty started the program some fifty years ago due to an addiction to alcohol he had in his twenties. Rusty towers over most, looking much younger than his actual age with the ability to kick anyone's butt in a pickup basketball game. Rusty attended AA meetings frequently with members from the group home affiliated with the center and joined residents many nights to have dinner together. Everyone knew they could always count on Rusty, day or night if they were struggling with their sobriety. He had been there. He knew exactly what it was like to have temptations, doubts, and weaknesses. As he often stated, "It's a daily struggle that I will have for the rest of my life."

Not more than a month after Gregg moved into the rehab residence while attending group meetings, he began noticing quirky, familiar mannerisms, and gestures by Rusty. These similar idiosyncrasies certainly gave him pause and moments of "Am I crazy?"—how

Rusty sat in a chair and crossed his long legs in a similar fashion to Gregg and most notably and alarming was how both held their index finger on the side of their face close to their ear with their middle finger touching the bridge of their nose. Now sober with an unfogged brain and crazy questions running through his mind, he decided to ask Rusty if they could talk after a meeting. Gregg, definitely nervous, just wanted to unburden himself and ask those questions before he lost his nerve. So he took a deep breath and asked Rusty if he was from upstate New York, specifically the Rochester area and if he ever worked at Kodak?

"Yes, I grew up in a suburb of Rochester and was employed at Kodak as a photographer before moving to Florida."

"Okay, great. Do you recall a woman named Kay from Rochester who also worked at Kodak?"

Rusty thought a minute then said, "Yes, I dated a woman named Kay right after I was divorced from my first wife in my early twenties. We vacationed several times together in Florida, but the relationship broke up as I wanted to move permanently to Florida, and as I recall, she wanted to return home to be near family. Why?"

Taking another deep breath, Gregg stated, "Kay is my birth mother, and I think you could be my father," then stepped back slightly, realizing the enormity of the moment.

"What? No...are you kidding me?" questioned Rusty.

It quickly became apparent that Rusty was standing in front of his biological son, and for the longest moment, all they did was stare at each other. Gregg literally, one month previously, walked into this treatment center that his undiscovered, until this moment, birth father started years ago—an amazing but true story.

Gregg would tell you that he believed it was fate that brought him to that center on that day, and it saved his life. They enjoyed a friendship and a unique support system from this unbelievable coincidence, if not complicated, until Rusty passed away early August 2019 at the age of ninety-four. Gregg has been clean and sober for over ten years—truly a miracle.

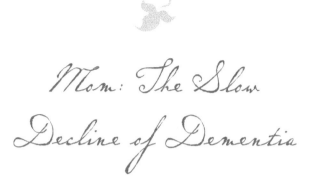

Mom: The Slow Decline of Dementia

I wish I had taken the opportunity to talk with my mother about what she thought was going on with her less than normal behavior. Was she aware of how confused she gets? Did she sense things were off but wanted to hide it? Was she scared? I'm not sure what she thought was happening to her sadly, as I never asked. There is a strange dynamic that happens between a parent and child when your roles reverse, when the mother becomes the child and the child becomes the adult. It's a new relationship that definitely takes time, patience, and many adjustments, but your parents are still your mother or your father regardless of their cognitive decline.

Her house was messy and unkempt. I'm not sure if she was eating properly, dressing appropriately, and I was terrified she would drive her car, get lost, or worse. Gregg took care of the car problem by letting the air out of one of her tires and told her that it had to be fixed before she could drive it. Amazingly, that seemed to work as each day she would gather her pocketbook, keys, and glasses and head to the garage as if to go to work. She would see the flat tire and tell Gregg that he had to get that tire fixed today as she couldn't take any more time off from work. This happened sporadically for a few more weeks until one day, she just stopped asking about both the car and the job.

I started in earnest to look at assisted living facilities near me in Massachusetts. Michigan was too far for me, and Gregg was too unsettled. Florida, where Curt lived, was never an option as I wanted her near me— just a daughter thing, I guess, but I thought I could do a better job overseeing my mom's physical and mental concerns than either of my brothers.

I found a recently renovated assisted living facility 8 miles from our home. It had been an old boutique-style hotel called the Merrimack Valley Motor Inn, run-down after years of neglect. They converted the two upper floors into apartments, and the third floor was designated as the memory care unit. The main entrance was bright and spacious, with couches and chairs scattered all around in soft, muted colors throughout the lobby. Sizable rooms on the main floor were converted into a music room, a library, a large gathering place with a piano, and a well-appointed dining room. After a tour and interview with the director of services, my mother was given a beautiful room on the second floor. It only had one window, but it was large and overlooking the beautifully landscaped grounds which sat on over five acres. I had my doubts that she should be on this independent floor but happily agreed with their evaluation and only requested that the kitchenette stove be turned off.

We moved her in on a beautiful Friday afternoon in late May and two days later I got a call from the director saying that my mother could not remain on the independent floor and needed to go to the memory care unit. As only one room was currently available, I needed to make a quick decision. I truly had no option, either move her upstairs or find another residence. I was definitely annoyed having just set her room up, trying to make it comfortable and cozy, and now I have to move her again just two days later. I totally understood their concerns and agreed with their new assessment, but it was difficult to see my mother with a little bit of panic and uncertainty in her eyes. Apparently, Mom got quite upset at dinner the night before as she was not allowed to save two seats at the dinner table for her parents, whom she stated were just running late.

It was a struggle and much anxiety for me, but she settled into her new apartment fairly quickly. She had a corner unit room with two large windows overlooking the parking lot, a twin bed, and her own bathroom. We bought a recliner in a soft teal color to match her bedspread and a wooden TV stand for her new television. I placed several framed photos around her room to make it feel homier. The memory care floor consisted of three pods, each containing a kitchen, a common dining area, and six individual bedrooms surrounding the shared space. For the first several years, she thought she was actually working. She would walk around with a clipboard and organize meetings all day long, whether it be an outing to the beach in which she would be wearing a bathing suit or to a restaurant for lunch in which she would be dressed appropriately with sweater and purse. It didn't matter that these events never occurred. She was always so convincing. One such incident replayed to me by one of the many caregivers was when my mother went around, telling everyone that "today is the day everyone gets to go home." Residents were emptying their closets and stacking up their belongings by the elevator. I gathered there was mayhem on the floor for hours.

I received a call early one Saturday morning from the director stating, "Ruthie is fine. I just have to let the families know when any incidents occur." On their 1:00 a.m. bed check, my mother was not in her room and after a frantic search she was finally located in Bill's room. He had the exact same room location as my mother, just in a different pod. I could hear the director was a little nervous telling the story, not knowing how I would react. Actually, all I could do was laugh, which was a great relief to her. They apparently were both found naked and awake. After putting her night-gown back on, they escorted my mother back to her room, tucked her in as she proceeded to fall fast asleep. I went to visit her the next day and found everyone in the common area playing with a beach ball. I pulled a chair up next to Mom, as she began telling me about each person sitting around that large circle. I was anxious to hear what she was going to say when we got to Bill as she clearly said, "I can't remember his name, but he's a big pain in the ass." You gotta laugh.

It was so bizarre to me that Mom had virtually no recollection of the last thirty years living in Michigan, but her memories growing up in Jamaica Estates, New York, a section of Queens, were clear and present. She often talked about her parents and how they were coming to visit soon. I, not comprehending the depth of her dementia, especially in the first couple of months as well as her ability to hide it so well, suggested we get a phone for her bedroom. I honestly thought I could call her like I did when she lived in Michigan. I received the first bill from the phone company after thirty days or so of her moving in. To my astonishment, there were well over three hundred calls to the same exact telephone number in Jamaica Estates, New York. There were pages and pages, and it was the only phone number ever called as she apparently had been trying to call her parents at her childhood phone number. I immediately called and canceled her phone services. I then called the number, hoping to offer an explanation and a sincere apology. However, when the phone was answered, I barely had time to say anything before this woman started yelling and swearing at me. At that point, I just hung up, unplugged the phone, and turned to my mother, saying that I needed to have the telephone repaired. She had an odd expression on her face and said, "Now you understand what I have been dealing with each day." Then we both just started laughing, the big-belly kind, each having no idea why the other one was laughing. It was cathartic.

She was confused easily and clearly had memory loss, but she still had that spunk and spirit in her being. Mom was well spoken, articulate, and often taken as a visitor rather than a resident. She introduced me as her sister but always called me Dale. There was a period over several years when Mom became obsessed with my father, often speaking about him being such an honest, decent man, and frequently mentioned how sexy she thought he was. On more than one occasion, a story was overheard and corroborated by a caregiver that my mother gleefully stated, "My Harry is a big man [wink, wink] in every way." Since my mother believed I was her sister and not her daughter, I think she felt free to share inappropriate stories that I really did not want to hear. Some was really funny, and some of it were heartbreaking.

My brother Curt came to visit Mom while she was still pretty mobile, and after having dinner at our home, he offered to return her to the assisted living facility, giving us a break from driving back and forth. Upon his return, he stormed into the house, clearly upset and barely able to explain what happened. On the drive back, my mother kept referring to Curt as Harry and kept rubbing her hand on his thigh and suggested they pull over. I thought it was hilarious, but he was mortified and said he would never ever *ever* get into a car with her alone again. Frank and I used to call it "fun with Alzheimer's," as Mom no longer had any filters. As the years passed and Mom became nonverbal and immobile, I began missing her more, especially all the quirky things she did and said that so irritated me as a child but appreciate and miss now.

Everyone knew Ruthie and always had such kind words to say about her. I am so grateful for all the wonderful care she received at that assisted living facility over the last twelve years. It truly is "the long goodbye." We sadly said our goodbyes on August 9, 2014. At age ninety-one and after living with dementia for fourteen years, she was finally with her Harry again.

Ruth at age 89

Dale: Fall Turning to Winter of 2015

It was late October when my brother Curt called me to say he got his results back from Ancestry.com as he had been looking for a more definitive ethnicity and any possible DNA matches. His ethnicity was spot on to what he had been told as a child, mostly Canadian, but there weren't any close DNA matches and, therefore, no one to contact to learn more about his heritage. I know this news or lack thereof was hard, as he was really looking for some kind of connection to his past with so many unanswered questions.

Since both my parents were gone, it made it easier for me to explore the new genealogy services. When growing up, Mom said she would be happy to help each of us locate a birth parent if we wanted or needed to although I'm not sure I ever truly believed her. After my mother and I overheard a conversation between Gregg and one of his sisters, we heard him say, "Okay, well tell Mom I said hello." It gave me a jolt and thought it was completely inappropriate and insensitive. Later that day Mom said to me, "I never thought I'd have to share any of you." That broke my heart.

Curiosity got me to order my own Ancestry.com kit. It was very easy—just spit in this little tube, shake it up, and send it back. Within a month, just before Christmas 2015, I got an e-mail confirming that my results were in. The ethnicity part was fascinating as I discovered I am 52 percent Irish, 29 percent Western European, and 9 percent Scandinavian. For my entire life, I thought I was half Dutch, half German. First surprise!

Unlike Curt's results, I had two close DNA hits. They matched it as a first or second cousin, and now my curiosity had really peaked. Could I possibly learn more about my heritage, blood relatives? Do I have any genetic siblings, and could I possibly find my birth parents? The thought was both exciting and terrifying, all at the same time.

Ancestry.com provides you with an e-mail address of any DNA matches, and I wrote to both of them, explaining that I was adopted and knew some basic information but nothing that was identifiable. I used most of the information obtained from the letter I received from the adoption agency in 2000. I reiterated that my birth mother was a twenty-two-year-old at the time of my birth and that she was a college graduate as were both of her parents. I also know she had a younger brother and that her dad was the president of a local bank.

From the letter, I knew my birth father was twenty-four, a college graduate, and had been in the Air Force. He had a sister, who was six years older, married with two children.

I also know that my birth parents met on a European cruise in the summer of 1953, had a shipboard romance and that my birth father did not know that I existed.

The first person to respond to me was a woman named Mardie, who is my birth mother's second cousin as her grandmother and my birth grandmother were sisters. Mardie was truly excited about me reaching out to her as she was very much into genealogy, frequently traveling to discover her ancestry. She was the perfect person to help me in this endeavor, and within three days, she had located whom she believed was my grandmother, Mary Fitzpatrick Davis. With that information, it took us less than a day to locate my birth mother, Ann Davis Butler.

At the same time, I received an email from a gentleman named Paul, a judge from Tennessee who is connected to me on my birth father's side. It was pure chance that each of my DNA hits happened to be one on the birth mother's side and one on my birth father's side. Paul, like Mardie, was interested in genealogy and had found my birth father within days of my initial e-mail. His name was John Stone but unfortunately passed away in September 2013. We easily located an obituary that listed a widow and three adult children. A residence in Florida was mentioned and included a picture of John. I thanked Paul for all his help but decided to put all my effort into my birth mother's side as I knew that she was still alive. Actually, I knew quite a bit about Ann Davis Butler. I knew she lived in upstate New York right outside of Albany, in the town of Glens Falls, New York. She was a widow, had two adult children, and had recently sold a condo in Naples, Florida. Frank found a picture of Ann on Facebook, and it was the first time I saw my birth mother as she looked to be enjoying an outdoor barbecue of some sort and was wearing a hat. I saw zero resemblance.

I also had a phone number.

Ann

I definitely needed a couple of days to process all this, even though I knew I had to contact her. I wanted some time to internalize this sudden and amazing information because I knew one way or another, my life was about to change forever. On the first Wednesday after New Year's Eve 2016, I finally got the courage to make the call. I dialed the number with my heart pounding so hard I was afraid I would not be able to speak. It rang and rang, and finally, a generic voice mail asked to leave a message. I hung up, feeling relieved and disappointed. I tried two more times that day and three times the next day. At this point, I was on an emotional roller coaster, realizing then that an eighty-four-year-old woman was probably not going to answer a number she did not recognize. So on this frigid Friday morning in January, I decided to leave a message. After the beep, I stated, "Hi, my name is Dale Virginia Foley, and I am looking for Ann Davis Butler. I understand that you need your privacy, but please let me know you received this message. Thank you."

I hung up and thought, *Well, that's it.* That was all I could really do. *Now just wait and see if someone actually calls back.* I was getting bundled up to take a walk around the neighborhood and clear my head as my phone rang. "Oh shit, oh shit, oh shit" was my immediate reaction. *This is it.* I answered, and the woman at the other end said, "I just received a strange message from this number, and I am Ann Davis Butler, and who are you?"

Oh shit, oh shit (silently this time).

I said, "My name is Dale Virginia Foley, and I was born June 1, 1954, and I think we may be related." There was literally a *gasp* and then "What? What? What?"

I think I blabbered on and on about Ancestry.com and the Internet. Obviously, it was a shocking moment for both of us, but Ann clearly more than me, as she had only thirty seconds to process this while I had three whole days.

My fear of her hanging up on me, or stating to never contact her again, didn't happen. We literally talked for over an hour and a half, and after the initial shock, Ann seemed quite interested in telling me all about her and her family.

I asked Ann who she thought she was calling back, and she said, "I thought it must be someone from Duke asking for money because I had used her maiden name of Davis."

Ann, that's what I have called her from our initial conversation as I thought Mrs. Butler was a bit formal, said that it crossed her mind not to return the phone call, but something just made her do it. She was extremely honest and open, expressing early on, "I guess I'm supposed to say I'm sorry, but I'm not. I did what I had to do."

That comment surprised me as it never occurred to me that I'd be looking for an apology. Not once did that ever cross my mind, maybe because I had a wonderful childhood. I just don't know. Sometime during our conversation, I asked about my birth father. I already knew she wouldn't have much information as the Spence Chapin letter stated she did not want him to know about her pregnancy, but I wasn't expecting her to say, "I can't even remember his name." I kind of chuckled and said his name was John Stone. She gasped again and said, "Oh my god, that is his name, and how do you know that?"

I explained I found him the same way I had found her through Ancestry.com but quickly let her know that he passed away in 2013 and never knew about me.

I'm sure on some level she was relieved she wasn't going to have to deal with him. Ann did tell me one of the few things she remembers about John was that he kept repeating, "I don't think my mother would like you." That's a strange comment from somebody you have a shipboard romance with.

Ann spoke a lot about her parents but especially her mother. She really admired her and talked fondly of their relationship. Similar to my mother, Mary's husband passed away at age fifty-seven and was a widow up until she died at age ninety-seven. Both were strong independent women. Mary Fitzpatrick Davis was said to be petite, with delicate features, quite attractive, as well as a talented artist having many shows of her work at various events. This flood of information was thrilling and definitely overwhelming all at the same time. It was an odd feeling talking about biological relatives. This was the first time I even talked to someone who was a blood relative other than my son. The only thing Ann was concerned about was how and when to tell her children. Having two grown children, Michael, her oldest, divorced, and currently living with her in New York and her daughter Polly, two years younger, married with one teenage son, all living in Utah.

I assured Ann I would never divulge my existence to either of them if that is her wish. She just needed time to figure out how to tell her children about me as she felt she lied to them. The only people who knew about me besides her husband Bill were her parents, brother, and an aunt and uncle, whom she told me she stayed with at the end of her pregnancy. This was the same aunt who helped her during my delivery and then the adoption. Ann told me then that it was Aunt Nannie, who actually named me as she had two sons and no daughters and always wanted a girl that she would name Virginia. And that's how I got the name. Just a mere coincidence that the name of my aunt, my mother's sister, is Virginia.

Bill and Ann made a conscious decision not to tell their children about me, and I don't think it (I) was ever discussed again.

Bill passed away in 2007 after a short illness, and Ann talked of how lonely she had been feeling. My sudden appearance came at a perfect time in her life but later confided to me that if Bill was still alive, she wasn't at all sure how he would react to me having found her.

We were nearing the end of our conversation, and she wanted some time to figure out how to tell her children this new and "exciting" revelation. This was going to be a difficult, if not complicated conversation with her children. So, literally, after an hour and a half of talking, we exchanged e-mail addresses. Immediately after I hung up I took a deep breath and tried to comprehend what just happened. Surreal keeps popping in my head as well as relief and maybe even a little disappointed. Disappointed in the fact that she did not ask me one question about my childhood. Nothing. During our conversation, I obviously brought up events in my life, but I found it interesting that she never asked one direct question regarding me, my childhood, where I lived or anything about my family life. I later found out she honestly did not think she had any right, even now some sixty years later. Once she signed the papers and handed me over to the agency, she rescinded all her authority, and moving forward, she no longer had any rights to information regarding me. Nor did it ever cross her mind to contact Spence Chapin to inquire about me. She closed the book and moved on. If I gave up a child, I would be incredibly curious as to what their life was like, but I don't think you can judge until you're in someone else's shoes. Maybe it was her defense mechanism. Funny, but it's almost as if we were talking about someone else's life, not mine. But mine it was.

I had not expected to hear back so soon, but Ann called the next afternoon to let me know she talked to both Polly and Michael, as well as several close friends. The floodgates were opening up, and this secret that she held for so very long was, all of a sudden, no longer a secret. I'm sure that was a difficult conversation to have with her children, but to her surprise and happiness, they both thought it was cool that they have a sister, albeit a half one.

Ann and I kept in touch through e-mail with an occasional phone call while Frank and I spent our first winter in our condo in Naples, Florida, from January through April 2016. It was a nice way to begin to get to know each other. How strange that just a couple of years earlier, Ann sold a condo she and Bill owned in Naples, Florida. Just one of the many crazy coincidences we have discovered about each other. Ann spent those long winter months in upstate New York, reflecting on her own life, gathering photos of her childhood, articles, news clippings of special moments or honors received and sent them to me in a large manila envelope. There was even an application form for me to register with the DAR, Daughters of the American Revolution. Ann told me she was "having so much fun gathering memories she hadn't thought of in a very long time." She intimated she had been quite lonely since Bill died, and this was a pleasant distraction while being housebound during this especially long cold winter.

Since I contacted Ann, many of my friends, coworkers, and family do not know what to call her—my first mother, my real mother, my other mother, my birth mother, or Ann. Ruth and Harry are my mother and father, mom and dad. Those are my parents, the ones that taught me about love and empathy, honesty, and family. They gave me stability and a wonderful childhood. My birth parents are just that, birth parents. I don't think that is disrespectful. It's just the truth or at least my truth.

So from the very first conversation we had, I have called my birth mother Ann.

Dale: Summer to Fall of 2016

After Mom passed away, Frank and I decided to put our home on the market. We lived there for thirty-three wonderful years, but it was clearly time to downsize as we didn't need all that room and expense, and with Mom gone, we no longer needed to live nearby. Downsizing to a condo on Cape Cod looked appealing, but first, we needed to sell our Andover home. We contacted a friend and neighbor, who was a real estate agent, and put a plan together. Remarkably, our house was on the market for only two weeks when we received multiple offers. Oh man, this is really happening. We had to move out in a little over two months, which seemed like an overwhelming task after years of accumulated stuff. We found a three-bedroom condo in Falmouth, Massachusetts, with beautiful views of Buzzards Bay in the distance and began looking forward to our next adventure on Cape Cod.

The transition from Andover to Falmouth was easy, especially with several close friends nearby who also downsized to the Cape. Truly amazed and blessed with a circle of friends that have been together for most of our adult lives. We have all been through marriages, children, weddings, funerals, bar mitzvahs, christenings, and vacation. I do know how lucky we are to have a close-knit group of friends, and the older I get, I realize just how rare these friendships can be.

One of those dear friends is Cathy, whom I met some forty years ago when she first started dating her now-husband Richard. Cathy grew up in a small rural town in upstate New York called Hudson Falls, which happens to be the town next to Glens Falls, where Ann raised her family and currently resides. Knowing I had recently connected with my birth mother, Cathy called her cousin Tim who was a prominent family court judge in Warren County, which incorporates Hudson Falls as well as Glens Falls, and asked him if, by chance, he knew an Ann Butler.

"Do you mean Ann Butler, who lives across the street from the park?"

Not only did he know Ann, but also knew her well and for many years. What? Cathy's first cousin knew my birth mother and had socialized together for well over thirty years. Just crazy. Ann frequently had a Fourth of July party at which Tim and his husband Michael were regulars, and she told me that Timmy was always the life of the party. His enthusiasm was contagious and always had wonderfully vivid stories. The first photo I saw of Ann on Facebook was at one of those parties. Tim's sister Maryellen and Ann were also good friends and tennis partners for almost thirty years. The coincidences, connections and crossed paths are mind boggling.

Tim sadly lost his battle with cancer and passed away late January 2016. Cathy, along with her husband Richard and sister and brother-in-law, all met Ann at Tim's funeral. I was thankful that Cathy took the time to seek Ann out during the reception at the Queensbury Inn after the service. Cathy thought she was "a lovely lady with warm, kind eyes." As the mourners were leaving the reception, Ann told Cathy she was so grateful she had come over to introduce herself during this sad occasion. It literally had only been three weeks since I contacted Ann, and even though Pandora's box was opened, the feelings and emotions were still very raw.

Cathy and Ann at Tim's service

During one of our phone conversations Ann mentioned that her brother Jim lives on Marco Island with his girlfriend, Phyllis, which is a short forty-five-minute drive from us. Jim and his first wife had been married for many years, raising their six daughters, but for reasons unknown to me, they separated and eventually divorced. All the girls were out of the house by then, either in college or living on their own. After being alone for several years, he met Phyllis through a friend of a friend. She was a couple of years younger than Jim and had been divorced for a long time. Jim, in his early eighties, was still active, playing golf and tennis several times a week, had a somewhat weathered but still handsome face, and a fit physique for his age.

They connected right away through a mutual love of golf and being outdoors, and he moved in with her within a year.

Since Jim and Phyllis lived so close, we decided to go and meet them for lunch on Marco Island. Surprisingly, I didn't feel nervous or anxious about meeting total strangers who happen to be my newfound family. Jim's daughter Sally answered the door, and as I did not know she was going to be there, I thought she was Phyllis. So naturally, I said, "Hi, you must be Phyllis," and Sally chuckled a little bit as she was about fifty-five years of age, and Phyllis was about seventy-five. I must say I did think Phyllis (Sally) looked damn good. I guess I was more nervous than I thought. Phyllis's condo was beautifully decorated in a beachy theme with spectacular views of the gulf. Introductions were made, and we all went to sit on the lanai while Phyllis served lemonade and iced tea. Jim was pretty quiet most of the afternoon, a trait normal for him, according to Ann, but the conversation among the three girls was comfortable and nonstop. Another "you can't make this stuff up" happened with Phyllis telling me she went to Lasell College and then moved to Andover, Massachusetts, when she first married. As I did. So much has transpired in my life since that initial phone call to Ann a mere eight months ago. I found and met my birth mother as well as both of my half siblings, spent our first winter in our new place in Florida, sold our home and our boat, purchased a condo on Cape Cod, and our son got engaged.

Ann and I were each trying to figure out this new relationship through conversations revealing each other's likes, dislikes, and just about everything in between. From our passion for the outdoors, love of reading, common political beliefs and tennis, to the more mundane, mutual dislike of corned beef and cabbage. Ann told me she had breast cancer at age seventy-one—left breast, lumpectomy, and radiation only. I also had left breast cancer but at age fifty-nine—lumpectomy and radiation only. I do believe most are coincidental, but it makes you wonder.

Wow, all these newfound facts were amazing to an adopted person. You were brought up your whole life without having any genetic background as every doctor's appointment started out with "I have no history as I was adopted." Suddenly, sixty-one years later, I had all this amazing information regarding *my* family history—some good, some bad, but all mine.

Ann and Dale: Spring of 2016

Frank and I returned home late April 2016 and made arrangements to go meet Ann, Polly, and Michael at her home in Glens Falls, New York, for the first time. We set a date for a weekend in mid-May that was good for everyone and booked a hotel in Glens Falls less than 2 miles from Ann's home. Polly was flying in from Utah, where she lives with her husband Jim and son James. She was the only one able to visit that weekend, but Michael would also be there as he was currently living with Ann. Frank and I set out on a beautiful summerlike Saturday in the middle of May and drove four hours to meet my birth mother and my half siblings face-to-face. I was definitely nervous and anxious as we neared Ann's house, but the fact that we talked, texted, and e-mailed for the last four months somewhat eased the awkwardness that was about to happen. As our GPS brought us directly to her driveway, I remember thinking, *Okay, let's get this over with*. As we approached the front door, it swung open, and Michael stepped outside, introduced himself, gave me a hug and shook

Frank's hand. Michael seemed like a genuinely nice guy and enthusiastic about our visit, instantly putting me at ease, which I thoroughly appreciated. I thought he looked very much like the pictures I had seen of his dad.

We followed Michael inside and glancing up a steep staircase abutting an electric chairlift, I saw Ann for the first time. After sixty-one years, it was hard to believe this reunion was about to happen. Uncharacteristically, I was not as emotional as I would have expected. Reaching the top of the stairs, I said, "Hi," and we hugged tightly for a moment, neither saying a word as I stepped aside allowing Michael and Frank to enter the room. The first five minutes were a little awkward, as you can imagine, with questions about our trip from Massachusetts, traffic, and the weather but soon settled into her living room as the conversation was more relaxed. Polly appeared and apologized for being late, which she wasn't. She had just gotten out of the shower as her shoulder-length light blond hair was wet, making her blouse damp at the shoulders. I liked Polly immediately. She was warm and engaging. Polly talked about her grandmother, Ann's mother, who only ever wanted to be referred to as Mary by her grandchildren, never Grandma or Nana. Through these stories, I got the impression that Mary was beloved by all her eight grandchildren. She sounded unique, independent, strong-willed, and ahead of her time. I wish I had gotten to meet her. They talked about living in New York City, raising two children, the summers spent on a boat in the Hamptons, moving to Glens Falls, owning a ski mountain, and much about everyone's current lives.

We literally talked for more than three hours. Exhausted, drained, and even a little energized, Frank and I decided to check into our hotel and get settled before going back to pick up Polly and Ann to go to dinner. Michael would not be joining us as he had to work but walked Frank and me outside to our car. As we descended down the steep staircase again, going through the garage this time, I noticed Ann's car. It was the exact model, year, and color as mine.

Frank and I stopped at the hotel bar for a quick glass of wine before heading out to dinner, as I think I needed that little extra fortitude. It really was so incredibly bizarre every time I stepped back and thought about whose house I was in and the conversations we had all afternoon.

Ann picked a quaint restaurant in the middle of town, and the four of us settled back, ordered wine, and continued where we left off in the afternoon, getting to know each other. As we were getting ready to leave the restaurant, Ann said, "I need to ask you two questions. Okay, religion and politics?"

I said, "Oh, that's easy, Protestant and Democrat." Both Polly and Ann smiled.

Ann had been planning a brunch the next morning at her home and invited several close friends to come over to meet Frank and me. She sent out a beautifully printed invitation, and fifteen of her friends enthusiastically replied yes. Upon arriving early I commented on how lovely her dining room looked, set up beautifully with flowers on card tables covered with white tablecloths, and thinking it was so sweet. Being someone that hates to be the center of attention, initially I felt somewhat awkward as guests started to arrive. Ann's friends turned out to be kind and so excited about our reunion. While driving back to Massachusetts, I had time to reflect on everything that happened in the last four and a half months. It amazes me how gracious and open Ann had become after keeping this secret for so many years.

John Stone

Over the course of the summer, Ann told me she was quite conflicted, with the notion that it was she that prevented me from ever knowing my birth father. I tried again to reassure her that I totally understood the decisions she made long ago and that John was deceased anyway. She was pretty adamant and told me that she had written a letter to John's widow and his three children, and she wanted me to read it before she sent it off. I was surprised and taken aback as she rarely ever talked about John. I thought it was touching and an admirable thing to do but certainly not necessary. I said as much to her, but she was steadfast in her determination to have this letter read by John Stone's family.

Another one of those *you can't make this shit up* was how I came about getting the address of John's widow, from his obituary dated September 2013, which listed a residence on the east coast of Florida. I mentioned this to Lauren, a close friend whom I've known since our early college days, and she told me one of her coworkers had a home in that part of Florida. "I'll ask him if he knows John Stone."

I said, "Great, yeah, sure." That was a shot in the dark, a needle in the haystack. Well...

Unbelievably, not only did he know John but also lived right next door to him and proceeded to tell Lauren that he had passed away a couple of years ago, but his widow was still living in that house.

And that's how I got the address so Ann could send this heartfelt letter to his widow and his three grown children.

This is the letter that Ann sent to John's family:

Dear Stone family,

I know this letter will be a very large shock to the four of you. Nevertheless, I hope you will read it, digest what I tell you, and respond to me.

I met John on a student tour of Europe in the summer of 1953. We had a brief affair during that tour, but by the time we returned to New York, we both knew we were not for each other, and we parted friends. However, in a fairly short time, I discovered I was pregnant but made the decision not to tell John.

I gave birth to a baby girl on June 1, 1954, and gave her up for adoption to an agency in New York. After that, I never heard anything from or about her until this past January when she called me. She had found me through Ancestry.com and a DNA match. She had also found John the same way.

She and I have spent the past five months getting to know each other and finally meeting face-to-face this past May. It has been a joy and a pleasure for both of us.

I now think it is time to contact the other half of her genetic family and, thus, this letter to the four of you. Please believe she and I want nothing from any of you, except information about health issues or anything else you think she might like to know. It would also be nice for her to receive pictures of any or all of you.

I am sorry John has died and couldn't receive this news—perhaps he would be pleased and forgive me for not letting him know about her. At the time, it was the right decision for me to make. These sixty years have changed that. You can contact me at Ann Davis Butler at adb****@gmail.com.

Several weeks had passed since Ann sent the letter and by now she fully expected to hear something, anything—but nothing. She waited a couple more days and then decided to resend it—return receipt requested, which required a signature. Four days later, Ann received the receipt back from the post office, stating it had been declined. Someone at that residence refused to sign and accept the letter. Ann was clearly upset that she was being ignored as she realized that John's widow had to have read that letter and assumed, as it turned out correctly, never contacted any of her three stepchildren.

So the ball was thrown back in Ann's court, clearly pissed she was not about to let this stop her. Her tenacity was amazing. I knew John's three children's names from the obituary and googled each one. We easily found an address in Georgia that we believed could be John's daughter. We obviously did not know if this was the correct woman, but Ann sent the letter that was declined by John's widow to this person in Georgia and kept her fingers crossed.

Several days later, Ann received a call from Margaret, and she was, in fact, the daughter of John Stone and the only other biological child of his as her younger brother and sister, were both adopted as infants. They talked for a short time before Margaret seemed to be having problems with her phone, which was cutting out and disconnecting, necessitating numerous callbacks. Ann called shortly after hanging up with Margaret, telling me she would likely be calling me that night. Apparently, Margaret was quite excited about this "shocking and intriguing" news, but as Ann mentioned, she thought Margaret seemed more distracted and somewhat louder after each call back. Sure enough, on that gorgeous summer evening, after having poured myself a glass of wine, my phone rang.

It was obvious immediately she was a little tipsy being both loud and excited, making it hard for me to fully understand what she was saying, especially with her heavy Southern accent. Margaret was most enthusiastic about our news and genuinely seemed interested in speaking to me, asking questions, and answering all of mine. She talked about her mother, who divorced John when the three kids were in their early twenties and how John met and married Joan a short time later. Apparently, no love lost between John's three children and their stepmother, to say the least.

Two sides to every story, but Margaret felt that Joan didn't care about anybody or anything except their dad and her own daughter. Margaret claimed Joan never attempted to get to know any of them and rarely spent any time together during the twenty-five years she was married to their dad. She told me ever since her dad's funeral, none of them had seen or heard from Joan. Margaret mentioned that Alice was very excited about Ann's letter as it piqued her curiosity about her own

ancestry and wanted to ask me about the whole process of how I actually found my birth mother. Sadly,
her brother John passed away the year after their dad
died from alcoholism, and Margaret choking up a bit,
stressed it had been a very rough couple of years. She
told me several times that her "daddy would have loved
me" in that thick Southern accent, which made me
laugh.

After thirty minutes or so, our conversation was
winding down and we exchanged e-mails with the
expectation of sending pictures to each other. Later
that evening, I found several photos of Frank, Alex,
and myself, which I e-mailed to her. Unfortunately,
that was the one and only time I have ever talked to
Margaret. I did send e-mails and left several messages
on her phone but have not heard from her since. Nor
did I ever hear from Alice. Very strange. I have no idea
what happened or have any knowledge of why she cut
off all communication. I am still hoping someday to
talk to her again, but truly, all I want is just a few pictures of her dad.

Several years later while editing this manuscript, my
curiosity peaked again. What happened? I just couldn't
fathom why I never heard from Margaret again. Was
she afraid I was after something or someone? Did she
doubt who I was? It made no sense, especially because
she showed such enthusiasm during our one and only

conversation. So I decided to text her one last time. This is the message I sent.

"Hi, Margaret, it's Dale Foley. We spoke several years ago after a letter you received from my birth mother Ann Davis Butler. I'm perplexed as to why I never heard from you after sending e-mails and texts. I certainly hope all is well, but truly all I would like is a picture of your dad in his thirties, forties, or fifties. I have included two pictures of my son and his wife, Keri. He doesn't really look like my husband's family, and I'm curious to see if Alex or myself resembles your dad. I want nothing else. I hope this finds you healthy and happy. Hoping to hear from you. Thanks."

I texted it twice, and it came back each time as undeliverable. I figured she had changed her phone number, but I decided to try one last time, and for some reason, this time, it went through. The next day, I heard from Margaret.

She texted, "Hi, Dale, I remember speaking to your mother several times. I forgot the whole story. Are you my father's daughter? Tell me again?"

Really? If someone called me, even years ago, and told me they were my half-sister, I think I would remember that conversation. This just seemed to get curiouser and curiouser.

So I texted back, "Yes, I am your father's biological daughter. I know that must sound so crazy. My birth mother Ann Davis had a shipboard romance in 1953 with your dad. I was conceived during that cruise, but he was never told. Fast forward sixty years, I contacted her through Ancestry.com and found your dad the same way. From the two pictures I sent, do you think my son looks like your dad?"

Margaret replied, "Is that your son in the picture with you? Or who is this of?"

I sent a picture of Alex and Keri, who were both thirty-four years old. I was truly now wondering what the hell was going on.

I then texted Margaret a picture of the four of us, Frank, myself, Alex, and Keri and sent it to her, explaining who everyone was.

She texted back, "This is all very interesting. I would like to know more. Maybe you can call me sometime," and included her phone number, which I already have because we've been texting. So I called her the next morning, and we spoke briefly as she was heading into a meeting. Appearing excited and interested to find out more, she stated she really had very little recollection of our conversation four years ago. Margaret told me she had not been feeling well for a long time due to arthritis and several back surgeries. She assured me she would send a picture of her dad that evening, but most of her pictures were in storage, and it would take some time for her to dig through them. Sure enough that night, I received a picture of John at his first wedding to Margaret's mother. She estimated him to be in his early thirties.

Keri, Alex, Dale and Frank

I texted her thanks and told her how much I appreciated the picture and thought they were a very handsome couple. I didn't really see a strong resemblance to my son, but other people have commented that they thought their smile was similar.

Margaret texted, "He was a very handsome decent gentleman. He always had strong ethics and integrity. I loved him very much. Probably too much. We should keep in touch. God bless."

That was the last time I heard from Margaret. I texted her several days before we were going to the east coast of Florida to visit some friends to see if we could meet somewhere for coffee as I know she lived close to our destination. She never responded to that text.

I then called her the morning before we were to head back and left a message. She did not answer my text, phone call or return my voice mail. I am at a complete loss. At least, I now have a picture.

John Stone - Early 30's

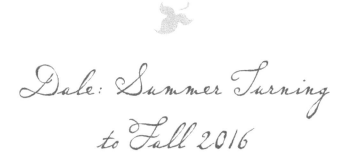

Dale: Summer Turning to Fall 2016

The summer was ramping up to be pretty hectic as we had to be out of our home by the end of August. Polly mentioned during brunch at her mom's house that she usually comes home for several weeks in late August as it's the only extended time off she gets between the summer job as an aquatic director at a Boy Scout camp and before ski season and would love to take a side trip to Massachusetts. Polly's husband Jim and their son James had never been to Massachusetts, and she thought it might be fun to see where we lived and to experience Boston. They all arrived on a beautiful but hot and humid late morning in August. Polly drove the four-hour trip with her husband Jim as copilot and in the back seat James and Grandma Ann. There were boxes and piles of junk all over our house, but nobody seemed to mind except me. Gathering around our dining table to eat lunch, the discussions were animated and varied. Everyone seemed comfortable and at ease even though it was our first time meeting Jim and James and only the second visit with Ann and Polly. We were all getting anxious to get to Boston, so we packed up and headed to the marina. They booked a couple of rooms in the Marriott Hotel in Charlestown next to the marina, where we would be staying on our boat, making it easier for Ann as walking any distance has become challenging.

They got settled in while Frank and I went to open the boat with plans to meet up shortly, but Ann texted that she was having back spasms and thought it best to just stay in the hotel and take a nap while the rest of the gang went off sightseeing. Dinner that night at a local seafood restaurant was more enjoyable than I anticipated. Still so incredibly weird. Hard to define exactly how I felt, but I was sure they were all analyzing me as I was doing the same of them.

The next morning, Polly, Jim, and James went off to do more exploring as we made plans to get together later that evening for dinner. This gave Ann, Frank, and myself some alone time together as she was planning to come to the boat late morning. I met Ann at the entrance to the marina just a short walk from her hotel lobby and suddenly realized just how difficult walking any distance was for her. As our boat was in the farthest slip from the entrance, we stopped several times along the way using the dock boxes as a sturdy bench to give Ann a rest and relieve the spasms. Lauren and her husband Harry were on their way to the marina to have lunch with us and, of course, to meet Ann. I could unequivocally state that without Lauren's persuasion over countless years, this reunion likely would not have happened. Lauren was absolutely the driving force for me in finding Ann (although Frank did all the legwork) as she was resolute in her determination to find out anything about my birth parents. I am now thankful for that.

It was a gorgeous balmy afternoon, and Ann and Lauren got along famously. Lauren, being the romantic she is, and curious about all things involving Ann and John, told her as much, and Ann, being a good sport, said, "Fire away." The afternoon was flying by, and I noticed Ann getting tired and suggested it might be time for me to bring her back to the hotel to get some rest before going out to dinner. Polly and her gang loved discovering all of what Boston has to offer as Ann, Frank and I enjoyed just getting to know more about each other.

Boston Duck Tour

The summer flew by as they so often do. Alex and Keri got engaged at the beginning of June, and we celebrated in New York City with Keri's parents. The rest of the summer was pretty much all about packing up, throwing out, and giving away.

Alex and Keri's wedding plans were in full swing now, even though the wedding wasn't going to take place until October 2017. The venue located in Saratoga Springs, New York, was doing a wedding tasting, something I had never heard of. Keri called and suggested it might be fun if her parents and Frank and I went with them to get an idea of how the wedding would look and feel. I loved the idea. Frank was unable to attend as he was traveling for work, so I asked Lauren. It was a perfect choice as she knew Alex's fiancé Keri and his future in-laws from Union College. It was actually Lauren and Harry's daughter Rachel who introduced Alex to Keri. Both Rachel and Keri went to Union College in Schenectady, New York, and a friendship developed through lacrosse. Rachel always thought of Alex as a younger brother and set them up on a blind date, and as they say, the rest is history.

I did not expect the luncheon to be like a real wedding but with over one hundred people it truly felt like one. We were all ushered into this beautiful hall with marble walls and ceilings rising so high it was difficult to see the ornately carved stonework. It was stunning with muted lighting and soft fabric draped beautifully along the sidewalls. On either side of the enormous dark oval-shaped bar were two hors d'oeuvre stations, one a seafood feast and the other a magnificent charcuterie table. Canapes seemed everywhere offered by tuxedo-clad men and women. The dessert station highlighting different types of wedding cakes, pastries and an ice cream bar were mouthwatering. My favorite was the cordial station with tiny chocolate cups to fill with your favorite aperitif. There was a large table located at the entrance with place cards in many different styles, indicating what table you were assigned.

After the hour-long cocktail reception, we were all escorted into the main dining room and located our beautifully set table with a gorgeous flower arrangement set in the middle. Each of us got to sample different salads, entrées, and desserts. It was really quite an event, albeit a major pig out, and I had no doubt that the upcoming wedding was going to be spectacular. Frank and I could not be happier, knowing that our only child found a best friend to share a life together who undeniably love and care for each other. We feel blessed to have her and her family in our lives.

Keri and Alex

Since Saratoga Springs, New York, is located just thirty minutes south of Glens Falls, Lauren and I invited ourselves to have dinner with Ann and Michael that evening. Several weeks prior, while making these plans, Ann asked me if I would drive her to Marshfield,

Massachusetts, on my way back home to the Cape as she wanted to visit an old friend from high school. I said absolutely and really didn't give it much thought until we were actually on our way. Ann had spent a little over a month at Spaulding rehabilitation center in Charlestown, Massachusetts, after having back surgery at Massachusetts General Hospital late fall of 2016. She reconnected with Chirp, yes, that Chirp, who was living in an assisted living facility in Marshfield, Massachusetts. He had been widowed for almost ten years. Even though they were unable to physically visit as Chirp no longer drove and Ann was rehabbing, they talked on the telephone daily, sometimes multiple times for hours on end as I was later told. After dropping Lauren off at her home in Needham, Ann and I headed to Marshfield. It was during this time that she fessed up to her reconnection with Chirp and talked of the many hours they spent on the phone, just getting to know one another again. It had been sixty-one years since they last saw one another, and interested, more like stunned, I asked what her plans were and when she would be returning home.

She said very nonchalantly, "I'm not quite sure, but Michael will probably pick me up in about two weeks." At that point, I *literally* burst out laughing, as did she, and I realized they *really* had reconnected. I was dropping Ann off to spend two weeks with her former fiancé that she hadn't seen in decades. What?

As we approached this beautifully landscaped assisted living facility set back and surrounded by nature, I could tell she was a little nervous. She got quiet and took out her compact and put on a little pink lipstick. While driving to Marshfield I stressed to Ann how insane this all seemed and said, "I must be the last person on the planet that Chirp would want to meet." Really, my head was spinning. She reassured me that that was not true, and Chirp was actually thrilled we had found each other. Are you kidding me? *I* am dropping off my birth mother to see the man she broke up with some sixty years ago because she was pregnant with me. That's not something that happens every day. The irony and completely, totally, bizarre occurrence did not escape me.

Chirp was waiting in the library just off the foyer of this lovely but slightly dated facility. As we entered, I knew right away it had to be Chirp as he stood up, pulled his sweater vest down, and seemed to dust off his pants with a huge smile planted on his face. He was quite tall but looked rather thin with a full head of straight grayish hair. I took Ann's suitcase from her and waited until she went over to greet him. As she walked over and hugged him, she then kind of nestled her head in his chest, similar to a toddler being shy and turning their head into their mom's body. Ann, with her head coming up to only his armpits, appeared vulnerable and adolescent. It was awkward to witness. They pulled apart from their embrace, and Ann waved me over. I extended my hand to Chirp in kind of a clumsy way, not really knowing how to greet him. He was very kind and put his other hand on top of mine, looking directly into my eyes and said how lovely it was to meet me.

At this point, I couldn't wait to get the hell out of there. He insisted that I come up to his apartment as he wanted to show me, as he stated, "Where your mother would be staying." Ugh, I wanted to say "not my mother", but Ann, but couldn't find my voice. He took the suitcase from my hand, and we all proceeded to the elevators at the end of the hall. We entered his small and sparsely furnished two-bedroom condo as Chirp proceeded to take Ann's suitcase to the back bedroom, which I never saw. After exiting the bedroom, Chirp showed me the small galley kitchen, the living room with a cream-colored sectional so low to the ground I couldn't imagine how either one of them would ever manage to get up off of it. The second bedroom had only a love seat, two small side tables that resembled the old TV dinner stackable tables, and the smallest television set I have ever seen nestled in the bookcase. I now *knew* they were "hooking up," as they say. Actually, I thought, ages eighty-five and eighty-six, good for them. Chirp was insistent on walking me to my car, and after saying my goodbyes to Ann, told her to call if she needed anything. As Chirp and I descended down the elevator, he thanked me for bringing Ann to him.

I thought Chirp was kind, thoughtful, engaging, and a true gentleman. I remember getting in the car, putting the directions in my GPS to get home, and thinking, *Oh my god! This is beyond crazy.*

The Nuptials

While Frank and I were spending our second winter in Florida, Ann called, wanting to know when we were coming home and if we were free on Saturday, May 13. I said, "Sure, we have no plans," assuming we were going to be invited to Glens Falls for a weekend visit. Actually, Ann was calling to invite Frank and me to her and Chirp's wedding, but more accurately, she was calling to invite me to be *in* her wedding.

Sixty-two years after Ann broke up with Chirp, they were finally going to be husband and wife.

I met Chirp's three children and their spouses the night before the wedding at a dinner hosted by Ann and Chirp for friends and family that were coming in from out of town.

They were married on Saturday, May 13, 2017, in a lovely old Episcopal church in the quintessentially New England town of Whitman, Massachusetts. The temperature was cool for a mid-May afternoon with a brilliant blue sky streaked with grayish-white clouds. The relatively small church had beautiful wooden pews and magnificent stained glass windows running up both sides. We were escorted into a room off the side of the back of the church where Colette, the minister, had us wait until everyone arrived. Colette was so excited with Ann's and my story and told me she felt so blessed to be able to marry as she stated, "A beautiful, loving couple in their late eighties." Polly and I were co-matrons of honor, and Michael walked his mother down the aisle. When Colette asked the congregation, "Who gives this woman away?"

Michael, in a clear, strong voice, said, "Me and my sisters." It still gives me pause.

It was a warm and touching ceremony as the bride looked radiant in a soft silvery dress. The irony did not escape me once again as I walked down the aisle side by side with Polly to witness my birth mother and the gentleman, whose heart she broke years ago, get married—truly amazing.

They had a small reception in the basement of the church, decorated tastefully with tablecloths and flower arrangements. They served white wine, lemonade, and finger sandwiches while friends and family from both sides mingled. It was the first time I actually met five of Chirp's nine grandchildren. His grandchildren were sweet and clearly just wanted their grandpa to be happy. To this day, I don't know if Chirp's children realize that I was the reason their dad and Ann didn't get married in 1954.

Dale and Polly at wedding

Ann and Michael at wedding

Ann and Chirp, the Happy Couple

About the Author

Dale Foley resides in Falmouth, Massachusetts, with her husband, Frank. Their son, Alex, is married and living in New York City. Creativity and joy define Dale and her passions are all connected by water. Her birth mother, and Dale's inspiration to write, started her long journey on a cruise ship. Fittingly, Dale lives on idyllic Cape Cod where she is never far from the sea. She spends her free time boating, participating in spirited water aerobics, and even cooking is often sous vide. Since COVID-19 interrupted the world, painting has become a pleasure and diversion while missing family and friends. Her specialty? Seascapes.

Dale Foley is a first time author.